U.S. Presbyterian Church

The Form of Government

the discipline, and the directory for worship of the Presbyterian Church in the

United States of America - as adopted, amended by the Presbyteries, and ratified

by the General Assembly, 1821-85

U.S. Presbyterian Church

The Form of Government
the discipline, and the directory for worship of the Presbyterian Church in the United States of America - as adopted, amended by the Presbyteries, and ratified by the General Assembly, 1821-85

ISBN/EAN: 9783337291808

Printed in Europe, USA, Canada, Australia, Japan

Cover: Foto ©Lupo / pixelio.de

More available books at **www.hansebooks.com**

THE
FORM OF GOVERNMENT,

THE

DISCIPLINE,

AND THE

DIRECTORY FOR WORSHIP,

OF THE

PRESBYTERIAN CHURCH

IN

THE UNITED STATES OF AMERICA,

AS ADOPTED, AMENDED BY THE PRESBYTERIES, AND RATIFIED BY THE GENERAL ASSEMBLY, 1821-85.

WITH THE RULES FOR JUDICATORIES.

PHILADELPHIA:
PRESBYTERIAN BOARD OF PUBLICATION,
No. 1334 Chestnut Street.

THE
FORM OF GOVERNMENT

AND

FORMS OF PROCESS

OF THE

PRESBYTERIAN CHURCH IN THE UNITED STATES OF AMERICA;

AS AMENDED AND RATIFIED BY THE GENERAL ASSEMBLY.

BOOK I.
OF GOVERNMENT.

CHAPTER I.
PRELIMINARY PRINCIPLES.*

THE Presbyterian Church in the United States of America, in presenting to the Christian public the system of union, and the form of government and discipline which they have adopted, have thought proper to state, by way of introduction, a few of the general principles by which they have been governed in the formation of the plan. This, it is hoped, will,

---

* NOTE.—This introductory chapter, with the exception of the first sentence, was first drawn up by the Synod of New York and Philadelphia, and prefixed to the Form of Government, &c., as published by that body in 1788. In that year, after arranging the plan on which the Presbyterian Church is now governed, the Synod was divided into four Synods, and gave place to the General Assembly which met for the first time in 1789

in some measure, prevent those rash misconstructions, and uncandid reflections, which usually proceed from an imperfect view of any subject; as well as make the several parts of the system plain, and the whole perspicuous and fully understood.

They are unanimously of opinion:

I. That "God alone is Lord of the conscience; and hath left it free from the doctrine and commandments of men, which are in any thing contrary to his word, or beside it in matters of faith or worship:" Therefore they consider the rights of private judgment, in all matters that respect religion, as universal and unalienable: they do not even wish to see any religious constitution aided by the civil power, further than may be necessary for protection and security, and, at the same time, be equal and common to all others.

II. That, in perfect consistency with the above principle of common right, every Christian church, or union or association of particular churches, is entitled to declare the terms of admission into its *communion*, and the qualifications of its ministers and members, as well as the whole system of its internal government which Christ hath appointed: that, in the exercise of this right, they may, notwithstanding, err, in making the terms of communion either too lax or too narrow; yet, even in this case, they do not infringe upon the liberty, or the rights of others, but only make an improper use of their own

III. That our blessed Saviour, for the edification of the visible church, which is his body, hath appointed officers, not only to preach the gospel *and administer the sacraments;* but also to exercise discipline, for the preservation both of truth and duty ; and, that it is incumbent upon these *officers*, and upon the whole church, in whose name they act, to censure or cast out the erroneous and scandalous ; observing. in *all* cases, the rules contained in the word of God.

IV. That truth is in order to goodness ; and the great touchstone of truth, its tendency to promote holiness ; according to our Saviour's rule, " by their fruits ye shall know them." And that no opinion can be either more pernicious or more absurd, than that which brings truth and falsehood upon a level, and represents it as of no consequence what a man's opinions are. On the contrary, they are persuaded that there is an inseparable connection between faith and practice, truth and duty. Otherwise it would be of no consequence either to discover truth, or to embrace it.

V. That while under the conviction of the above principle, they think it necessary to make effectual provision, that all who are admitted as teachers, be sound in the faith ; they also believe that there are truths and forms, with respect to which men of good characters and principles may differ. And in all these they think t. the duty both of private Christians and societies, to exercise mutual forbearance towards each other.

VI. That though the character, qualifications, and authority of church officers, are laid down in the holy Scriptures, as well as the proper method of their investiture and institution; yet the election of the persons to the exercise of this authority, in any particular society, is in that society.

VII. That all church power, whether exercised by the body in general, or in the way of representation by delegated authority, is only ministerial and declarative; *that is to say*, that the Holy Scriptures are the only rule of faith and manners; that no church judicatory ought to pretend to make laws, to bind the conscience in virtue of their own authority; and that all their decisions should be founded upon the revealed will of God. Now though it will easily be admitted, that all synods and councils may err, through the frailty inseparable from humanity; yet there is much greater danger from the usurped claim of making laws, than from the right of judging upon laws already made, and common to all who profess the gospel; although this right, as necessity requires in the present state, be lodged with fallible men.

VIII. *Lastly.* That, if the preceding scriptural and rational principles be steadfastly adhered to, the vigour and strictness of its discipline will contribute to the glory and happiness of any church. Since ecclesiastical

FORM OF GOVERNMENT. 409

discipline must be purely moral or spiritual in its object, and not attended with any civil effects, it can derive no force whatever, but from its own justice, the approbation of an impartial public, and the countenance and blessing of the great Head of the church universal.

CHAPTER II.
OF THE CHURCH.

I. JESUS CHRIST, who is now exalted far above all principality and power,[a] hath erected, in this world, a kingdom, which is his church.[b]

II. The universal church consists of all those persons, in every nation, together with their children who make profession of the holy religion of Christ, and of submission to his laws.[c]

[a] Eph. i. 20, 21. When he raised him from the dead, and set him at his own right hand in the heavenly places, far above all principality, and power, and might, and dominion, and every name that is named, not only in this world, but also in that which is to come. Psa. lxviii. 18. Thou hast ascended on high, thou hast led captivity captive: thou hast received gifts for men ; yea, for the rebellious also, that the Lord God might dwell among them.

[b] Psa. ii. 6. Yet have I set my king upon my holy hill of Zion. Dan. vii. 14 —There was given him dominion, and glory, and a kingdom, that all people, nations, and languages, should serve him ; his dominion is an everlasting dominion, which shall not pass away, and his kingdom that which shall not be destroyed. Eph. i. 22, 23. And hath put all things under his feet, and gave him to be the head over all things to the church, which is his body, the fulness of him that filleth all in all.

[c] Rev. v. 9. And hast redeemed us to God by thy

III As this immense multitude cannot meet together in one place, to hold communion, or to worship God, it is reasonable, and warranted by Scripture example, that they should be divided into many particular churches.[d]

IV. A particular church consists of a number of professing Christians, with their offspring, voluntarily associated together, for divine worship and godly living, agreeably to the Holy Scriptures;[e] and submitting to a certain form of government.[f]

---

blood out of every kindred, and tongue, and people, and nation. Acts ii. 39. For the promise is unto you, and to your children, and to all that are afar off, even as many as the Lord our God shall call. 1 Cor. i. 2, compared with 2 Cor. ix. 13.

[d] Gal. i. 21, 22. Afterwards I came into the regions of Syria and Cilicia: and was unknown by face unto the churches of Judea which were in Christ. Rev. i. 4, 20. John to the seven churches which are in Asia: Grace be unto you, and peace, from him which is, and which was, and which is to come: and from the seven spirits which are before his throne.—The mystery of the seven stars which thou sawest in my right hand, and the seven golden candlesticks. The seven stars are the angels of the seven churches; and the seven candlesticks which thou sawest are the seven churches. See also Rev. ii. 1.

[e] Acts ii. 41, 47. Then they that gladly received his word were baptized; and the same day there were added unto them about three thousand souls. Praising God, and having favour with all the people. And the Lord added to the church daily such as should be saved. 1 Cor. vii. 14. For the unbelieving husband is sanctified by the wife, and the unbelieving wife is sanctified by the husband; else were your children unclean; but now are they holy. Acts ii. 39. Mark x. 14, compared with Matt. xix. 13, 14, and Luke xviii. 15, 16.

[f] Heb. viii. 5. Who serve unto the example and

CHAPTER III.

OF THE OFFICERS OF THE CHURCH.

I. Our blessed Lord at first collected his church out of different nations,^f and formed it into one body,^h by the mission of men endued with miraculous gifts, which have long since ceased.ⁱ

II. The ordinary and perpetual officers in the church are Bishops, or Pastors;^j the

---

shadow of heavenly things, as Moses was admonished of God when he was about to make the tabernacle; for, See (saith he) that thou make all things according to the pattern showed to thee in the mount. Gal. vi. 16. And as many as walk according to this rule, peace be on them, and mercy, and upon the Israel of God.

f Psa. ii. 8. Ask of me, and I shall give thee the heathen for thine inheritance, and the uttermost parts of the earth for thy possession. Rev. vii. 9. After this, I beheld, and lo, a great multitude, which no man could number, of all nations, and kindreds, and people, and tongues, stood before the throne, and before the Lamb, clothed with white robes, and palms in their hands.

h 1 Cor. x. 17. For we, being many, are one bread, and one body: for we are all partakers of that one bread. See also Eph. iv. 16. Col. ii. 19.

i Matt. x. 1, 8. And when he had called unto him his twelve disciples, he gave them power against unclean spirits, to cast them out, and to heal all manner of sickness, and all manner of disease, &c.

j 1 Tim. iii. 1. If a man desire the office of a bishop, he desireth a good work. Eph. iv. 11, 12. And he gave some, apostles; and some, prophets; and some, evangelists; and some, pastors and teachers; for the perfecting of the saints, for the work of the ministry for the edifying of the body of Christ.

representatives of the people, usually styled Ruling Elders;[k] and Deacons.[l]

CHAPTER IV.

OF BISHOPS OR PASTORS.

THE pastoral office is the first in the church, both for dignity and usefulness.[m] The person who fills this office, hath, in Scripture, obtained different names expressive of his various duties. As he has the oversight of the flock of Christ, he is termed bishop.*[n] As he feeds them with spiritual food, he is termed pastor.[o] As he serves Christ in his church, he is termed minister.[p] As it is his duty to be grave and

---

[k] 1 Tim. v. 17. Let the elders that rule well, be counted worthy of double honour.

[l] Phil. i. 1. To all the saints in Christ Jesus which are at Philippi, with the bishops and deacons.

[m] Rom. xi. 13.

[n] Acts xx. 28. Take heed therefore, unto yourselves, and to all the flock over the which the Holy Ghost hath made you overseers, [bishops] to feed the church of God, which he hath purchased with his own blood.

[o] Jer. iii. 15. And I will give you pastors according to mine heart, which shall feed you with knowledge and understanding. 1 Pet. v. 2, 3, 4.

[p] 1 Cor. iv. 1. Let a man so account of us, as of the ministers of Christ, and stewards of the mysteries of

---

* As the office and character of the gospel minister is particularly and fully described in the Holy Scriptures, under the title of bishop; and as this term is peculiarly expressive of his duty as an overseer of the flock, it ought not to be rejected.

prudent, and an example of the flo k, and to govern well in the house and kingdom of Christ, he is termed presbyter or elder.^q As he is the messenger of God, he is termed the angel of the church.^r As he is sent to declare the will of God to sinners, and to beseech them to be reconciled to God through Christ, he is termed ambassador.^s And, as he dispenses the manifold grace of God, and the ordinances instituted by Christ, he is termed steward of the mysteries of God.^t

CHAPTER V.

OF RULING ELDERS.

RULING elders are properly the representa-

God. 2 Cor. iii. 6. Who also hath made us able ministers of the New Testament.

q 1 Pet. v. 1. The elders which are among you I exhort, who am also an elder, and a witness of the sufferings of Christ, and also a partaker of the glory that shall be revealed. See also Tit. i. 5. 1 Tim. v. 1, 17, 19.

r Rev. ii. 1. Unto the angel of the church of Ephesus write. Rev. i. 20.—The seven stars are the angels of the seven churches. See also Rev. iii. 1, 7. Mal. ii. 7.

s 2 Cor. v. 20. Now then we are ambassadors for Christ, as though God did beseech you by us; we pray you, in Christ's stead, be ye reconciled to God. Eph. vi. 20.

t Luke xii. 42. Who then is that faithful and wise steward, whom his lord shall make ruler over his household to give them their portion of meat in due season? 1 Cor iv. 1, 2.—Moreover, it 's req ired in stewards that a man be found faithful.

tives of the people, chosen by them for the purpose of exercising government and discipline, in conjunction with pastors or ministers.ᵘ This office has been understood, by a great part of the Protestant Reformed Churches, to be designated in the holy Scriptures, by the title of governments; and of those who rule well, but do not labour in the word and doctrine.ᵛ

CHAPTER VI.

OF DEACONS.

THE Scriptures clearly point out deacons as distinct officers in the church,ʷ whose business it is to take care of the poor, and to distribute among them the collections which may be raised for their use.ˣ To them also may be properly committed the ma-

---

ᵘ 1 Tim. v. 17. Let the elders that rule well be counted worthy of double honour, especially they who labour in the word and doctrine. Rom. xii. 7, 8. Acts xv. 25.

ᵛ 1 Cor. xii. 28. And God hath set some in the church, first, apostles; secondarily, prophets; thirdly, teachers; after that miracles; then gifts of healings, helps, governments, diversities of tongues. See letter (*u*) above.

ʷ Phil. i. 1. 1 Tim. iii. 8 to 15.

ˣ Acts vi. 1, 2. And in those days, when the number of the disciples was multiplied, there arose a murmuring of the Grecians against the Hebrews, because their widows were neglected in the daily ministration. Then the twelve called the multitude of the disciples unto them, and said, It is not reason that we should leave the word of God and serve tables.

ɩ ɪgement of the temporal affairs of the church.ʸ

CHAPTER VII.
OF ORDINANCES IN A PARTICULAR CHURCH.

THE ordinances established by Christ, the head, in a particular church, which is regularly constituted with its proper officers,ᵃ are prayer,ᵃ singing praises,ᵇ reading,ᶜ expounding and preaching the word of God;ᵈ

ʸ Acts vi. 3, 5, 6. Wherefore, brethren, look ye out among you seven men of honest report, full of the Holy Ghost and wisdom, whom we may appoint over this business.—And the saying pleased the whole multitude: and they chose Stephen, a man full of faith and of the Holy Ghost, and Philip, and Prochorus, and Nicanor, and Timon, and Parmenas. and Nicolas, a proselyte of Antioch: whom they set before the apostles: and when they had prayed, they laid their hands on them.

ᵃ 1 Cor. xiv. 26, 33, 40. Let all things be done unto edifying.—For God is not the author of confusion, but of peace, as in all churches of the saints.—Let all things be done decently, and in order.

ᵃ Acts vi. 4. But we will give ourselves continually to prayer, and to the ministry of the word. 1 Tim. ii. 1.

ᵇ Col. iii. 16. Teaching and admonishing one another in psalms, and hymns, and spiritual songs, singing with grace in your hearts to the Lord. Psa. ix. 11. Eph. v. 19 Also Col. iv. 16.

ᶜ Acts xv. 21. Luke iv. 16, 17.

ᵈ Titus i. 9 Holding fast the faithful word as he hath been taught, that he may be able by sound doctrine both to exhort and convince the gainsayers. Acts x. 42 —He commanded us to preach unto the people. See also Acts ·xviii. 23 Luke xxiv 47. 2 Tim iv 2. Acts ix. 20

administering baptism and the Lord's supper;[e] public solemn fasting and thanksgiving,[f] catechizing,[g] making collections for the poor and other pious purposes;[h]

---

[e] Matt. xxviii. 19, 20. Go ye, therefore, and teach all nations, baptizing them in the name of the Father, and of the Son, and of the Holy Ghost, &c. And Mark xvi. 15, 16. 1 Cor. xi. 23, 24, 25, 26. For I have received of the Lord, that which also I delivered unto you, that the Lord Jesus, the same night in which he was betrayed, took bread: and when he had given thanks, he brake it, and said, Take, eat; this is my body, which is broken for you: this do in remembrance of me. After the same manner also, he took the cup, when he had supped, saying, This cup is the New Testament in my blood: this do ye, as oft as ye drink it, in remembrance of me. For as often as ye eat this bread, and drink this cup, ye do show the Lord's death till he come. Compared with 1 Cor. x. 16.

[f] Luke v. 35. But the days will come, when the bridegroom shall be taken away from them, and then shall they fast in those days. Psa. l. 14. Offer unto God thanksgiving: and pay thy vows unto the Most High. Phil. iv. 6.—In every thing, by prayer and supplication, with thanksgiving, let your requests be made known unto God. See 1 Tim. ii. 1. Psa. xcv. 2.

[g] Heb. v. 12. For when for the time ye ought to be teachers, ye have need that one teach you again, which be the first principles of the oracles of God; and are become such as have need of milk, and not of strong meat.

[h] 1 Cor. xvi. 1, 2, 3, 4. Now concerning the collection for the saints, as I have given order to the churches of Galatia, even so do ye. Upon the first day of the week let every one of you lay by him in store, as God hath prospered him, that there be no gatherings when I come. And when I come, whomsoever ye shall approve by your letters, them will I send to bring your liberality unto Jerusalem. And if it be meet that I go also, they shall go with me. Gal. ii. 10. Only they would that we should remember the poor; the same which I also was forward to do.

exercising discipline;¹ and blessing the people.ʲ

CHAPTER VIII.

OF CHURCH GOVERNMENT, AND THE SEVERAL KINDS OF JUDICATORIES.

I. It is absolutely necessary that the government of the church be exercised under some certain and definite form.ᵏ And we hold it to be expedient, and agreeable to Scripture and the practice of the primitive Christians, that the church be governed by congregational, presbyterial, and synodical assemblies. In full con-

---

ⁱ Heb. xiii. 17. Obey them that have the rule over you, and submit yourselves: for they watch for your souls, as they that must give account; that they may do it with joy, and not with grief: for that is unprofitable for you. 1 Thess. v. 12, 13. And we beseech you, brethren, to know them which labour among you, and are over you in the Lord, and admonish you; and to esteem them very highly in love for their work's sake. And be at peace among yourselves.

ʲ 2 Cor. xiii. 14. The grace of the Lord Jesus Christ, and the love of God, and the communion of the Holy Ghost, be with you all. Amen. Eph. i. 2. Grace be to you, and peace from God our Father, and from the Lord Jesus Christ.

ᵏ Ezek. xliii. 11, 12. Show them the form of the house, and the fashion thereof, and the goings-out thereof, and the comings-in thereof, and all the forms thereof, and all the ordinances thereof, and all the forms thereof, and all the laws thereof: and write it in their sight that they may keep the whole form thereof, and all the ordinances thereof, and do them. This is the law of the

sistency with this belief, we embrace, in the spirit of charity, those Christians who differ from us, in opinion and practice, on these subjects.[l]

II. These assemblies ought not to possess any civil jurisdiction, nor to inflict any civil penalties.[m] Their power is wholly moral or spiritual, and that only ministerial and declarative.[n] They possess the right of requiring obedience to the laws of Christ; and of excluding the disobedient and disorderly from the privileges of the church. To give efficiency, however, to this necessary and scriptural authority, they possess the powers requisite for obtaining evidence and inflicting censure. They can call before them any offender against the order and government of the church; they can require members of their own society to appear and give testimony in the cause; but the highest punishment to which their authority extends, is to exclude the contumacious and impenitent from the congregation of believers.[o]

---

[l] Acts xv. 5, 6. But there rose up certain of the sect of the Pharisees, which believed, saying, That it was needful to circumcise them, and to command them to keep the law of Moses. And the apostles and elders came together for to consider of this matter.

[m] Luke xii. 13, 14. And one of the company said unto him, Master, speak to my brother, that he divide the inheritance with me. And he said unto him, Man, who made me judge or a divider over you? John xviii. 36.—My kingdom is not of this world.

[n] Acts xv. from the 1st to the 32d verse.

[o] Matt. xviii. 15, 16, 17, 18, 19, 20. Moreover, if thy brother shall trespass against thee, go and tell him

CHAPTER IX.
OF THE CHURCH SESSION.

I. THE Church session consists of the pastor or pastors, and ruling elders, of a particular congregation.^p

II. Of this judicatory, two elders, if there be as many in the congregation, with the pastor, shall be necessary to constitute a quorum.

III. The pastor of the congregation shall always be the moderator of the session; except when, for prudential reasons, it may appear advisable that some other minister should be invited to preside; in which case the pastor may, with the concurrence of the session, invite such other minister as they may see meet, belonging to the same presbytery, to preside in

---

his fault between thee and him alone: if he shall hear thee, thou hast gained thy brother. But if he will not hear thee, then take with thee one or two more, that in the mouth of two or three witnesses every word may be established. And if he shall neglect to hear them, tell it unto the church: but if he neglect to hear the church, let him be unto thee as a heathen man and a publican. Verily I say unto you, Whatsoever ye shall bind on earth, shall be bound in heaven: and whatsoever ye shall loose on earth, shall be loosed in heaven. 1 Cor v. 4, 5. In the name of our Lord Jesus Christ, when ye are gathered together, and my spirit, with the power of our Lord Jesus Christ, to deliver such an one unto Satan, for the destruction of the flesh, that the spirit may be saved in the day of the Lord Jesus.

p 1 Cor. v. 4. In the name of our Lord Jesus Christ, when ye are gathered together, and my spirit, with the power of our Lord Jesus Christ

that case. The same expedient may be adopted in case of the sickness or absence of the pastor.

IV. It is expedient, at every meeting of the session, more especially when constituted for judicial business, that there be a presiding minister. When, therefore, a church is without a pastor, the moderator of the session shall be, either the minister appointed for that purpose by the presbytery, or one invited by the session to preside on a particular occasion. But where it is impracticable, without great inconvenience, to procure the attendance of such a moderator, the session may proceed without it.

V. In congregations where there are two or more pastors, they shall, when present, alternately preside in the session.

VI. The Church session is charged with maintaining the spiritual government of the congregation;[q] for which purpose, they have power to inquire into the knowledge and Christian conduct of the members of the church;[r] to call before them offenders and witnesses, being members of their own congregation, and to introduce other witnesses, where it may be necessary to bring the process to issue, and when they can be procured to attend; to receive members into the church; to

---

[q] Heb. xiii. 17. Obey them that have the rule over you, and submit yourselves: for they watch for your souls, as they that must give account; that they may do it with joy, and not with grief. 1 Thss. v. 12, 13, and 1 Tim. v. 17.

[r] Ezek. xxxiv. 4.

admonish, to rebuke, to suspend, or exclude from the sacraments, those who are found to deserve censure;^s to concert the best measures for promoting the spiritual interests of the congregation; and to appoint delegates to the higher judicatories of the church.^t

VII. The pastor has power to convene the session when he may judge it requisite;^u and he shall always convene them when requested to do so by any two of the elders. The session shall also convene when directed so to do by the presbytery.

VIII. Every session shall keep a fair record of its proceedings; which record shall be, at least once in every year, submitted to the inspection of the presbytery.

IX. It is important that every church session keep a fair register of marriages; of baptisms, with the times of the birth of the individuals baptized; of persons admitted to the Lord's table, and of the deaths, and other removals of church members.

---

^s 1 Thess. v. 12, 13. And we beseech you, brethren, to know them which labour among you, and are over you in the Lord, and admonish you; and to esteem them very highly in love for their work's sake. And be at peace among yourselves. See also 2 Thess. iii. 6, 14, 15. 1 Cor. xi. 27 to the end.

^t Acts xv. 2, 6. When therfore Paul and Barnabas had no small dissension and disputation with them, they determined that Paul and Barnabas, and certain other of them, should go up to Jerusalem unto the apostles and elders, about this question.—And the apostles and elders came together for to consider of this matter.

^u Acts. xx. 17.

CHAPTER X.

OF THE PRESBYTERY.

1. THE Church being divided into many separate congregations, these need mutual counsel and assistance, in order to preserve soundness of doctrine, and regularity of discipline, and to enter into common measures for promoting knowledge and religion, and for preventing infidelity, error, and immorality.ᵛ Hence arise the importance and usefulness of presbyterial and synodical assemblies.ʷ

II. A presbytery consists of all the ministers, in number not less than five, and one ruling elder from each congregation, within a certain district.

III. Every congregation, which has a stated

ᵛ The church of Jerusalem consisted of more than one, as is manifest both before and after the dispersion, from Acts vi. 1, 6. Acts ix. 31. Acts xxi. 20. Acts ii. 41, 46, 47, and iv. 4. These congregations were under one presbyterial government, proved from Acts xv. 4. Acts xi. 22, 30. Acts xxi. 17, 18. Acts vi. That the church of Ephesus had more congregations than one, under a presbyterial government, appears from Acts xix. 18 19, 20. 1 Cor. xvi. 8, 9, 19, compared with Acts xviii. 19, 24, 26. Acts xx. 17, 18, 25, 28, 30, 31, 36, 37. Rev. ii 1, 2, 3, 4, 5, 6.

ʷ 1 Tim. iv. 14. Neglect not the gift that is in thee, which was given thee by prophecy, with the laying on of the hands of the presbytery. Acts xv. 2, 3, 4, 6, 22.—And when they were come to Jerusalem, they were received of the church, and of the apostles and elders, and they declared all things that God had done with them.—And the apostles and elders came together for to consider of this matter.

pastor has a right to be represented by one elder; and every collegiate church by two or more elders, in proportion to the number of its pastors.

IV. Where two or more congregations are united under one pastor, all such congregations shall have but one elder to represent them.

V. Every vacant congregation, which is regularly organized, shall be entitled to be represented by a ruling elder in presbytery.

VI. Every elder not known to the presbytery, shall produce a certificate of his regular appointment from the church which he represents.[x]

VII. Any three ministers, and as many elders as may be present belonging to the presbytery, being met at the time and place appointed, shall be a quorum competent to proceed to business.[y]

VIII. The presbytery has power to receive

---

[x] Acts xv. 1, 2, 3, 4, 5, 6. 1 Cor. xiv. 26, 33, 40.—Let all things be done unto edifying;—for God is not the author of confusion, but of peace, as in all churches of the saints.—Let all things be done decently and in order.

[y] Acts xiv. 26, 27. And thence sailed to Antioch, from whence they had been recommended to the grace of God for the work which they fulfilled. And when they were come, and had gathered the church together, they rehearsed all that God had done with them, and how he had opened the door of faith unto the Gentiles. Compared with Acts xi. 18. When they heard these things, they held their peace, and glorified God, saying, Then hath God also to the Gentiles granted repentance unto life.

and issue appeals from church sessions ⁱ and references brought before them in an orderly manner;ᵃ to examine and license candidates for the holy ministry;ᵇ to ordain, instal, remove, and judge ministers;ᶜ to examine and approve or censure the records of church sessions; to resolve questions of doctrine or discipline seriously and reasonably proposed;ᵈ to

---

ⁱ Acts xv. 5, 6, 19, 20. But there rose up certain of the sect of the Pharisees, which believed, saying, that it was needful to circumcise them, and to command them to keep the law of Moses. And the apostles and elders came together for to consider of this matter.—Wherefore my sentence is, that we trouble not them which from among the Gentiles are turned to God: but that we write unto them, that they abstain from pollutions of idols, and from fornication, and from things strangled, and from blood.

ᵃ Acts xviii. 24, 27. And a certain Jew named Apollos, born at Alexandria, an eloquent man, and mighty in the Scriptures, came to Ephesus.—And when he was disposed to pass into Achaia, the brethren wrote, exhorting the disciples to receive him. Compared with Acts xix. 1, 2, 3, 4, 5, 6, 7.

ᵇ 1 Tim. iv. 14. Neglect not the gift that is in thee which was given thee by prophecy, with the laying on of the hands of the presbytery. Acts xiii. 2, 3. As they ministered to the Lord, and fasted, the Holy Ghost said, Separate me Barnabas and Saul, for the work whereunto I have called them. And when they had fasted and prayed, and laid their hands on them they sent them away.

ᶜ Acts xv. 28. For it seemed good to the Holy Ghost, and to us, to lay upon you no greater burdens than these necessary things. 1 Cor. v. 3.

ᵈ Acts xv. 10. Now, therefore, why tempt ye God, to put a yoke upon the neck of the disciples, which neither our fathers nor we were able to bear? Compared with Gal. ii. 1. 6.

condemn erroneous opinions which injure the purity or peace of the church;ᵉ to visit particular churches, for the purpose of inquiring into their state, and redressing the evils that may have arisen in them;ᶠ to unite or divide congregations, at the request of the people, or to form or receive new congregations, and in general to order whatever pertains to the spiritual welfare of the churches under their care.ᵍ

IX. It shall be the duty of the presbytery to keep a full and fair record of their proceed-

---

ᵉ Acts xv. 22, 23, 24. Then pleased it the apostles and elders, with the whole church, to send chosen men of their own company to Antioch with Paul and Barnabas; namely, Judas surnamed Barsabas, and Silas, chief men among the brethren: and they wrote letters by them after this manner. The apostles, and elders, and brethren, send greeting unto the brethren which are of the Gentiles in Antioch, and Syria, and Cilicia: forasmuch as we have heard that certain which went out from us have troubled you with words, subverting your souls, saying, Ye must be circumcised, and keep the law; to whom we gave no such commandment.

ᶠ Acts xx. 17. And from Miletus he sent to Ephesus, and called the elders of the church. Acts vi. 2. Then the twelve called the multitude of the disciples unto them, and said, It is not reason that we should leave the word of God, and serve tables. Acts xv. 30. So when they were dismissed, they came to Antioch; and when they had gathered the multitude together, they delivered the epistle.

ᵍ Eph. vi. 18. Praying always with all prayer and supplication in the Spirit, and watching thereunto with all perseverance and supplication for all saints.—Phil. iv. 3. Be careful for nothing: but in every thing by prayer and supplication, with thanksgiving, let your requests be made known unto God.

ings, and to report to the synod, every year, licensures, ordinations, the receiving or dismissing of members, the removal of members by death, the union or division of congregations, or the formation of new ones; and in general, all the important changes which may have taken place within their bounds in the course of the year.

X. The presbytery shall meet on its own adjournment; and when any emergency shall require a meeting sooner than the time to which it stands adjourned, the moderator, or, in case of his absence, death, or inability to act, the stated clerk, shall, with the concurrence, or at the request of two ministers and two elders, the elders being of different congregations, call a special meeting. For this purpose he shall send a circular letter, specifying the particular business of the intended meeting, to every minister belonging to the presbytery, and to the session of every vacant congregation, in due time previous to the meeting; which shall not be less than ten days. And nothing shall be transacted at such special meeting besides the particular business for which the judicatory has been thus convened.

XI. At every meeting of presbytery, a sermon shall be delivered, if convenient; and every particular session shall be opened and closed with prayer.

XII. Ministers in good standing in other

presbyteries, or in any sister churches, who may happen to be present, may be invited to sit with the presbytery, as corresponding members. Such members shall be entitled to deliberate and advise, but not to vote in any decisions of the presbytery.

CHAPTER XI.

OF THE SYNOD.*

I. As a presbytery is a convention of the bishops and elders within a certain district, so a synod is a convention of the bishops and elders within a larger district, including at least three presbyteries. The synod may be composed, at its own option, with the consent of a majority of its presbyteries, either of all the bishops and an elder from each congregation in its district, with the same modifications as in the presbytery, or of equal delegations of bishops and elders, elected by the presbyteries on a basis and in a ratio determined in like manner by the synod itself and its presbyteries.

II. Any seven ministers, belonging to the synod, who shall convene at the time and place of meeting, with as many elders as may be present, shall be a quorum to transact synodical business; provided not more than three of the said ministers belong to one presbytery.

III. The same rule, as to corresponding members, which was laid down with respect to the presbytery, shall apply to the synod.

---

* As the proofs already adduced in favour of a presbyterial assembly in the government of the church, are equally valid in support of a synodical assembly, it is unnecessary to repeat the scriptures to which reference has been made under Chap. X., or to add any other.

IV. The synod has power to receive and issue all appeals regularly brought up from presbyteries, *provided*, that in the trial of judicial cases the synod shall have power to act by commission, in accordance with the provisions on the subject of judicial commissions in the Book of Discipline; to decide all references made to them; its decisions on appeals, complaints, and references, which do not affect the doctrine or constitution of the church, being final; to review the records of presbyteries, and approve or censure them; to redress whatever has been done by presbyteries contrary to order; to take effectual care that presbyteries observe the constitution of the church; to erect new presbyteries, and unite or divide those which were before erected; generally to take such order with respect to the presbyteries, sessions, and people under their care, as may be in conformity with the word of God and the established rules, and which tend to promote the edification of the church; and, finally, to propose to the General Assembly, for their adoption, such measures as may be of common advantage to the whole church.

V. The synod shall convene at least once in each year; at the opening of which a sermon shall be delivered by the moderator, or, in case of his absence, by some other member; and every particular session shall be opened and closed with prayer.

VI. It shall be the duty of the synod to keep full and fair records of its proceedings, to submit them annually to the inspection of the General Assembly, and to report to the Assembly the number of its presbyteries, and of the members and alterations of the presbyteries.

CHAPTER XII.

OF THE GENERAL ASSEMBLY.*

I. THE General Assembly is the highest judicatory of the Presbyterian Church. It shall represent, in one body, all the particular churches of this denomination; and shall bear the title of THE GENERAL ASSEMBLY OF THE PRESBYTERIAN CHURCH IN THE UNITED STATES OF AMERICA.

II. The General Assembly shall consist of an equal delegation of bishops and elders from each presbytery, in the following proportion; viz: each presbytery consisting of not more than twenty-four ministers, shall send one minister and one elder; and each presbytery consisting of more than twenty-four ministers, shall send one minister and one elder for each

---

* The radical principles of Presbyterian church government and discipline are:—That the several different congregations of believers, taken collectively, constitute one church of Christ, called emphatically the church;—that a larger part of the church, or a representation of it, should govern a smaller, or determine matters of controversy which arise therein;—that, in like manner, a representation of the whole should govern and determine in regard to every part, and to all the parts united; that is, that a majority shall govern: and consequently that appeals may be carried from lower to higher judicatories, till they be finally decided by the collected wisdom and united voice of the whole church. For these principles and this procedure, the example of the apostles, and the practice of the primitive church, are considered as authority. See Acts xv. to the 29th verse: and the proofs adduced under the last three chapters.

twenty-four ministers, or for each additional fractional number of ministers not less than twelve; and these delegates, so appointed, shall be styled, Commissioners to the General Assembly.

III. Any fourteen or more of these commissioners, one half of whom shall be ministers, being met on the day, and at the place appointed, shall be a quorum for the transaction of business.

IV. The General Assembly shall receive and issue all appeals, complaints, and references that affect the doctrine or constitution of the Church, which may be regularly brought before them from the inferior judicatories; *provided*, that in the trial of judicial cases the General Assembly shall have power to act by commission, in accordance with the provisions on the subject of judicial commissions in the Book of Discipline. They shall review the records of every synod, and approve or censure them: they shall give their advice and instruction in all cases submitted to them in conformity with the constitution of the Church; and they shall constitute the bond of union, peace, correspondence, and mutual confidence, among all our churches.

V. To the General Assembly also belongs the power of deciding in all controversies respecting doctrine and discipline; of reproving, warning, or bearing testimony against error in doctrine, or immorality in practice, in any church, presbytery, or synod; of erecting new synods when it may be judged necessary; of superintending the concerns of the whole Church; of corresponding with foreign churches, on such terms as may be agreed upon by the Assembly and the corresponding body; of suppressing schismatical contentions and disputations; and, in general, of recommending and attempting reformation, of manners, and the promotion of charity, truth. and holiness, through all the churches under their care.

VI. Before any overtures or regulations proposed by the Assembly to be established as constitutional rules, shall be obligatory on the churches, it shall be necessary to transmit them to all the presbyteries, and to receive the returns of at least a majority of them, in writing, approving thereof.

VII. The General Assembly shall meet at least once in every year. On the day appointed for that purpose, the moderator of the last Assembly, if present, or in case of his absence, some other minister, shall open the meeting with a sermon, and preside until a new moderator be chosen. No commissioner shall have a right to deliberate or vote in the Assembly, until his name shall have been enrolled by the clerk, and his commission examined, and filed among the papers of the Assembly.

VIII. Each session of the Assembly shall be opened and closed with prayer. And the whole business of the Assembly being finished, and the vote taken for dissolving the present Assembly, the moderator shall say from the chair,—"By "virtue of the authority delegated to me, by "the church, let this General Assembly be dis- "solved, and I do hereby dissolve it, and re- "quire another General Assembly, chosen in "the same manner, to meet at "on the   day of   A. D.   "—

after which he shall pray and return thanks, and pronounce on those present the apostolic benediction.

CHAPTER XIII.

OF ELECTING AND ORDAINING RULING ELDERS AND DEACONS.

I. HAVING defined the officers of the church, and the judicatories by which it shall be governed, it is proper here to prescribe the mode in which ecclesiastical rulers should be ordained to their respective offices, as well as some of the principles by which they shall be regulated in discharging their several duties.

II. Every congregation shall elect persons to the office of ruling elder, and to the office of deacon, or either of them, in the mode most approved and in use in that congregation.[b] But in all cases the persons elected must be male members in full communion in the church in which they are to exercise their office.

III. When any person shall have been elected to either of these offices, and shall have declared his willingness to accept thereof, he shall be set apart in the following manner:

IV. After sermon, the minister shall state, in a concise manner, the warrant and nature of the office of ruling elder or deacon, together with the character proper to be sustained, and the duties to be fulfilled by the officer elect

---

[b] 1 Cor. xiv. 40.

having done this, he shall propose to the candidate, in the presence of the congregation, the following questions :—viz.

1. Do you believe the Scriptures of the Old and New Testaments to be the word of God, the only infallible rule of faith and practice?

2. Do you sincerely receive and adopt the confession of faith of this church, as containing the system of doctrine taught in the Holy Scriptures?

3. Do you approve of the government and discipline of the Presbyterian church in these United States?

4. Do you accept the office of ruling elder (or deacon, as the case may be) in this congregation, and promise faithfully to perform all the duties thereof?

5. Do you promise to study the peace, unity, and purity of the church?

The elder, or deacon elect, having answered these questions in the affirmative, the minister shall address to the members of the church the following question :—viz.

Do you, the members of this church, acknowledge and receive this brother as a ruling elder, (or deacon) and do you promise to yield him all that honour, encouragement, and obedience, in the Lord, to which his office, according to the word of God, and the constitution of this church, entitles him?

The members of the church having answered this question in the affirmative, by holding up their right hands, the minister shall proceed to set apart the candidate, by prayer, to the office of ruling elder, (or deacon, as the [1] case may be) and shall give to him, and to the congregation, an exhortation suited to the occasion.

V. Where there is an existing session, it is proper that the members of that body, at the close of the service, and in the face of the congregation, take the newly ordained elder by the hand, saying in words to this purpose,—" We " give you the right hand of fellowship, to take " part of this office with us."

VI. The offices of ruling elder and deacon are both perpetual, and cannot be laid aside at pleasure. No person can be divested of either office but by deposition. Yet an elder or deacon may become, by age or infirmity, incapable of performing the duties of his office; or he may, though chargeable with neither heresy nor immorality, become unacceptable, in his official character, to a majority of the congregation to which he belongs. In either of these cases he may, as often happens with respect to a minister, cease to be an acting elder or deacon.

VII. Whenever a ruling elder or deacon, from either of these causes, or from any other, not inferring crime, shall be incapable of serving the church to edification, the session shall take order on the subject, and state the fact, together with the reasons of it, on their records. *Provided always*, that nothing of this kind shall be done without the concurrence of

---

[1] Acts vi. 5, 6.

the individual in question, unless by the advice of presbytery.

VIII. If any particular church, by a vote of members in full communion, shall prefer to elect ruling elders for a limited time in the exercise of their functions, this may be done; *provided*, the full time be not less than three years, and the session be made to consist of three classes, one of which only shall be elected every year; and *provided*, that elders, once ordained, shall not be divested of the office when they are not re-elected, but shall be entitled to represent that particular church in the higher judicatories, when appointed by the session or the presbytery

CHAPTER XIV.
OF LICENSING CANDIDATES OR PROBATIONERS TO PREACH THE GOSPEL

I. THE Holy Scriptures require that some trial be previously had of them who are to be ordained to the ministry of the gospel, that this sacred office may not be degraded, by being committed to weak or unworthy men;[j] and that the churches may have an opportunity to form a better judgment respecting the talents of those by whom they are to be instructed and governed. For this purpose presbyteries shall license probationers to preach the gospel, that after a competent trial of their talents, and receiving from the churches a good report,

---
[j] 1 Tim. iii. 6. 2 Tim. ii. 2.

they may, in due time, ordain them to the sacred office.[k]

II. Every candidate for licensure shall be taken on trials by that presbytery to which he most naturally belongs; and he shall be considered as most naturally belonging to that presbytery within the bounds of which he has ordinarily resided. But in case any candidate should find it more convenient to put himself under the care of a presbytery at a distance from that to which he most naturally belongs, he may be received by the said presbytery, on his producing testimonials either from the presbytery within the bounds of which he has commonly resided, or from any two ministers of that presbytery in good standing, of his exemplary piety, and other requisite qualifications.

III. It is proper and requisite that candidates applying to the presbytery to be licensed to preach the gospel, produce satisfactory testimonials of their good moral character, and of their being regular members of some particular church. And it is the duty of the presbytery, for their satisfaction with regard to the real piety of such candidates, to examine them respecting their experimental acquaintance with religion, and the motives which influence them to desire the sacred office.[l] This examination shall be close and particular, and, in most cases, may best be conducted in the

---

[k] 1 Tim. iii. 7.   1 John 12.
[l] Rom. ii. 21, in connection with letter (*j*), page 435.

presence of the presbytery only. And it is recommended that the candidate be also required to produce a diploma of bachelor or master of arts, from some college or university: or, at least, authentic testimonials of his having gone through a regular course of learning.

IV. Because it is highly reproachful to religion, and dangerous to the church, to intrust the holy ministry to weak and ignorant men,^m the presbytery shall try each candidate, as to his knowledge of the Latin language; and the original languages in which the Holy Scriptures were written. They shall also examine him on the arts and sciences; on theology, natural and revealed; and on ecclesiastical history, the sacraments, and church government. And in order to make trial of his talents to explain and vindicate, and practically to enforce, the doctrines of the gospel, the presbytery shall require of him,

1. A Latin exegesis on some common head in divinity.

2. A critical exercise; in which the candidate shall give a specimen of his taste and judgment in sacred criticism; presenting an explication of the original text, stating its connection, illustrating its force and beauties, removing its difficulties, and solving any important questions which it may present.

3. A lecture, or exposition of several verses of scripture; and,

4. A popular sermon.

---

m See letter (*j*), and (*k*), pages 435, 436.

V. These, or other similar exercises, at the discretion of the presbytery, shall be exhibited until they shall have obtained satisfaction as to the candidate's piety, literature, and aptness to teach in the churches.ⁿ The lecture and popular sermon, if the presbytery think proper, may be delivered in the presence of a congregation.

VI. That the most effectual measures may be taken to guard against the admission of insufficient men into the sacred office,º it is recommended that no candidate, except in extraordinary cases, be licensed, unless, after his having completed the usual course of academical studies, he shall have studied divinity at least two years, under some approved divine or professor of theology.

VII. If the presbytery be satisfied with his trials, they shall then proceed to license him in the following manner: The moderator shall propose to him the following questions: viz.

1. Do you believe the Scriptures of the Old and New Testaments to be the word of God, and only infallible rule of faith and practice?

2. Do you sincerely receive and adopt the confession of faith of this church, as containing the system of doctrine taught in the Holy Scriptures?

3. Do you promise to study the peace, unity, and purity of the church?

ⁿ Tim. iii. 2 —Apt to teach. See also the foregoing quotations.

See letter 'j) page 435.

4. Do you promise to submit yourself, in the Lord, to the government of this presbytery, or of any other presbytery in the bounds of which you may be called?

VIII. The candidate having answered these questions in the affirmative, and the moderator having offered up a prayer suitable to the occasion, he shall address himself to the candidate to the following purpose:—" In the name " of the Lord Jesus Christ, and by that autho- " rity which he hath given to the church for ' its edification, we do license you to preach ' the gospel, wherever God in his providence ' may call you: and for this purpose, may the '' blessing of God rest upon you. and the Spirit " of Christ fill your heart.—*Amen.*'" and reco 'd shall be made of the licensure in the following or like form : viz.

At   the   day of
  the presbytery of having received testimonials in favour of
of his having gone through a regular course of literature; of his good moral character; and of his being in the communion of the church; proceeded to take the usual parts of trial for his licensure: and he having given satisfaction as to his accomplishments in literature ; as to his experimental acquaintance with religion ; and as to his proficiency in divinity and other studies; the presbytery did, and hereby do, express their approbation of al! these parts of trial and he having adopted

the confession of faith of this church, and satisfactorily answered the questions appointed to be put to candidates to be licensed; the presbytery did, and hereby do license him, the said ———— to preach the Gospel of Christ, as a probationer for the holy ministry, within the bounds of this presbytery, or wherever else he shall be orderly called.

IX. When any candidate for licensure shall have occasion while his trials are going on, to remove from the bounds of his own presbytery into those of another, it shall be considered as regular for the latter presbytery, on his producing proper testimonials from the former to take up his trials at the point at which they were left, and conduct them to a conclusion, in the same manner as if they had been commenced by themselves.

X. In like manner, when any candidate, after licensure, shall, by the permission of his presbytery, remove without its limits, an extract of the record of his licensure, accompanied with a presbyterial recommendation, signed by the clerk, shall be his testimonials to the presbytery under whose care he shall come.

XI. When a licentiate shall have been preaching for a considerable time, and his services do not appear to be edifying to the churches, the presbytery may, if they think proper, recall his license.

CHAPTER XV.

OF THE ELECTION AND ORDINATION OF BISHOPS OR PASTORS, AND EVANGELISTS.

I. When any probationer shall have preached so much to the satisfaction of any congregation, as that the people appear prepared to elect a pastor, the session shall take measures to convene them for this purpose: and it shall always be a duty of the session to convene them, when a majority of the persons entitled to vote in the case, shall, by a petition, request that a meeting may be called.

II. When such a meeting is intended, the session shall solicit the presence and counsel of some neighbouring minister to assist them in conducting the election contemplated, unless highly inconvenient on account of distance; in which case they may proceed without such assistance.

III. On a Lord's-day, immediately after public worship, it shall be intimated from the pulpit, that all the members of that congregation are requested to meet on   ensuing. at the church, or usual place for holding public worship; then and there, if it be agreeable to them, to proceed to the election of a pastor for that congregation.

IV. On the day appointed, the minister invited to preside, if he be present, shall, if it be deemed expedient, preach a sermon; and after sermon he shall announce to the people, that he will immediately proceed to take the votes of the electors of that congregation, for a pastor, if such be their desire: and when this desire shall be expressed by a majority of voices, he shall then proceed to take votes accordingly. In this election, no person shall be entitled to vote who refuses to submit to the censures of the church, regularly administered; or who does not contribute his just proportion, according to his own engagements, or the rules of that congregation, to all its necessary expenses.

V. When the votes are taken, if it appear that a large minority of the people are averse from the candidate who has a majority of votes, and cannot be induced to concur in the call, the presiding minister shall endeavour to dissuade the congregation from prosecuting it further. But if the people be nearly, or entirely, unanimous; or if the majority shall insist upon their right to call a pastor, the presiding minister, in that case, after using his utmost endeavours to persuade the congregation to unanimity, shall proceed to draw a call, in due form, and to have it subscribed by the electors; certifying at the same time, in writing, the number and circumstances of those who do not concur in the call: all which proceedings shall be laid before the presbytery, together with the call.

VI. The call shall be in the following or like form: viz.

The congregation of   being, on sufficient grounds, well satisfied of the ministerial qualifications of you   and having good hopes, from our past experience of your labours, that your ministrations in the Gospel will be profitable to our spiritual interests, do earnestly call and desire you to undertake the pastoral office in said congregation; promising you, in the discharge of your duty, all proper support, encouragement, and obedience in the Lord. And that you may be free from worldly cares and avocations, we hereby promise and oblige ourselves to pay to you the sum of   in regular quarterly (or half yearly, or yearly) payments, during the time of your being and continuing the regular pastor of this church. In testimony whereof, we have respectively subscribed our names, this   day of   A. D.

Attested by A. B., Moderator of the meeting.

VII. But if any congregation shall choose to subscribe their call by their elders and deacons, or by their trustees, or by a select committee, they shall be at liberty to do so. But it shall, in such case, be fully certified to the presbytery, by the minister, or other person who presided, that the persons signing have been appointed, for this purpose, by a public vote of the congregation; and that the call has been, in all other respects, prepared as above directed.

VIII. When a call shall be presented to any minister or candidate, it shall always be viewed as a sufficient petition from the people for his instalment. The acceptance of a call, by a minister or candidate, shall always be considered as a request, on his part, to be installed at the same time. And when a candidate shall be ordained in consequence of a call from any congregation, the presbytery shall, at the same time, if practicable, install him pastor of that congregation.

IX. The call, thus prepared, shall be presented to the presbytery, under whose care the person called shall be; that, if the presbytery think it expedient to present the call to him, it may be accordingly presented: and no minister or candidate shall receive a call but through the hands of the presbytery.

X. If the call be to a licentiate of another presbytery, in that case the commissioners deputed from the congregation to prosecute the call, shall produce, to that judicatory, a certificate from their own presbytery, regularly attested by the moderator and clerk, that the call has been laid before them, and that it is in order. If that presbytery present the call to their licentiate, and he be disposed to accept it, they shall then dismiss him from their jurisdiction, and require him to repair to that presbytery, into the bounds of which he is called; and there to submit himself to the usual trials preparatory to ordination.

XI. Trials for ordination, especially in a different presbytery from that in which the candidate was licensed, shall consist of a careful examination as to his acquaintance with experimental religion; as to his knowledge of philosophy, theology, ecclesiastical history, the Greek and Hebrew languages, and such other branches of learning as to the presbytery may appear requisite; and as to his knowledge of the constitution, the rules and principles of the government, and discipline of the church; together with such written discourse, or discourses, founded on the word of God, as to the presbytery shall seem proper.[p] The presbytery, being fully satisfied with his qualifications for the sacred office, shall appoint a day for his ordination, which ought to be, if convenient, in that church of which he is to be the minister. It is also recommended that a fast day be observed in the congregation previous to the day of ordination.[q]

XII. The day appointed for ordination being come, and the presbytery convened, a member of the presbytery, previously appointed to that duty, shall preach a sermon adapted to the occasion. The same, or another member appointed to preside, shall afterwards briefly recite from the pulpit, in the audience of the people, the proceedings of the presbytery preparatory to this transaction: he shall point out the nature and importance of the ordinance; and endeavour to impress the audience with a proper sense of the solemnity of the transaction.

Then addressing himself to the candidate,

---

p See the proofs in sections 1, 2, 3 4, of chapter iv.

q Acts xiii. 2, 3.

he shall propose to him the following questions, viz:

1. Do you believe the Scriptures of the Old and New Testaments to be the word of God, the only infallible rule of faith and practice?[r]

2. Do you sincerely receive and adopt the confession of faith of this church, as containing the system of doctrine taught in the Holy Scriptures?[s]

3. Do you approve of the government and discipline of the Presbyterian Church in these United States?[t]

4. Do you promise subjection to your brethren in the Lord?[u]

5. Have you been induced, as far as you know your own heart, to seek the office of the holy ministry from love to God, and a sincere desire to promote his glory in the gospel of his Son?[v]

6. Do you promise to be zealous and faithful in maintaining the truths of the gospel, and the purity and peace of the church; whatever persecution or opposition may arise unto you on that account?[w]

7. Do you engage to be faithful and diligent in the exercise of all private and personal du-

---

[r] 2 Tim iii. 16. Eph. ii. 20
[s] 2 Tim. i. 13.
[t] See letter (s) above.
[u] 1 Pet. v. 5.
  1 Cor. ii. 2. 2 Cor. iv. 5.
[v] Acts xx. 17 to 31.

ties, which become you as a Christian and a minister of the gospel; as well as in all relative duties, and the public duties of your office; endeavouring to adorn the profession of the gospel by your conversation; and walking with exemplary piety before the flock over which God shall make you overseer?[x]

8. Are you now willing to take the charge of this congregation, agreeably to your declaration at accepting their call? And do you promise to discharge the duties of a pastor to them, as God shall give you strength?[y]

XIII. The candidate having answered these questions in the affirmative, the presiding minister shall propose to the people the following questions:—

1. Do you, the people of this congregation, continue to profess your readiness to receive   whom you have called to be your minister?

2. Do you promise to receive the word of truth from his mouth, with meekness and love; and to submit to him in the due exercise of discipline?[s]

3. Do you promise to encourage him in his arduous labour, and to assist his endeavours for your instruction and spiritual edification?[a]

4. And do you engage to continue to him,

---

[x] See the epist'es to Timothy and Titus throughout.
[y] 1 Pet. v. 2.
[s] James i. 21. Heb. xiii. 17.
[a] 1 Thess. v. 12, 13.

while he is your pastor, that competent worldly maintenance which you have promised; and whatever else you may see needful for the honour of religion, and his comfort among you?[b]

XIV. The people having answered these questions in the affirmative, by holding up their right hands, the candidate shall kneel down in the most convenient part of the church. Then the presiding minister shall, by prayer,[c] and with the laying on of the hands of the presbytery,[d] according to the apostolic example, solemnly ordain him to the holy office of the gospel ministry. Prayer being ended, he shall rise from his knees; and the minister who presides shall first, and afterward all the members of the presbytery in their order, take him by the right hand, saying, in words to this purpose, "We give you the right hand of fellowship, to "take part of this ministry with us."[e] After which the minister presiding, or some other appointed for the purpose, shall give a solemn charge in the name of God, to the newly ordained bishop,[f] and to the people,[g] to persevere in the discharge of their mutual duties; and shall then, by prayer, recommend them

---

[b] 1 Cor. ix. 7 to 15.
[c] Acts xiii. 2, 3.
[d] 1 Tim. iv. 14.
[e] Gal. ii. 9. Acts i. 25
[f] 2 Tim iv. 1, 2.
[g] Mark iv. 24. Heb ii 1 See also letters (y), (s), and (z), page 447

both to the grace of God, and his holy keeping, and finally, after singing a psalm, shall dismiss the congregation with the usual blessing. And the presbytery shall duly record the transaction.

XV. As it is sometimes desirable and important that a candidate who has not received a call to be the pastor of a particular congregation, should, nevertheless, be ordained to the work of the gospel ministry, as an evangelist to preach the gospel, administer sealing ordinances, and organize churches, in frontier or destitute settlements; in this case, the last of the preceding questions shall be omitted, and the following used as a substitute:—viz.

Are you now willing to undertake the work of an evangelist; and do you promise to discharge the duties which may be incumbent on you in this character, as God shall give you strength?

CHAPTER XVI.

OF TRANSLATION, OR REMOVING A MINISTER FROM ONE CHARGE TO ANOTHER.

I. No bishop shall be translated from one church to another, nor shall he receive any call for that purpose, but by the permission of the presbytery.

II. Any church, desiring to call a settled minister from his present charge, shall, by commissioners properly authorized, represent to the presbytery the ground on which they plead his removal. The presbytery, having maturely considered their plea, may, according as it appears more or less reasonable, either recommend to them to desist from prosecuting the call, or may order it to be delivered to the minister to whom it is directed. If the parties be not prepared to have the matter issued at that presbytery, a written citation shall be given to the minister and his congregation, to appear before the presbytery at their next meeting. This citation shall be read from the pulpit in that church, by a member of the presbytery appointed for that purpose, immediately after public worship; so that at least two Sabbaths shall intervene betwixt the citation and the meeting of the presbytery at which the cause of translation is to be considered. The presbytery being met, and having heard the parties, shall, upon the whole view of the case, either continue him in his former charge, or translate him, as they shall deem to be most for the peace and edification of the church; or refer the whole affair to the synod at their next meeting, for their advice and direction.

III. When the congregation calling any settled minister is within the limits of another presbytery, that congregation shall obtain leave from the presbytery to which they belong, to apply to the presbytery of which he is a member and that presbytery, having cited him and his congregation as before directed, shall proceed to hear and issue the cause. If they agree to the translation, they shall release him from his present charge; and having given him proper testimonials, shall require him to repair to that presbytery, within the bounds of which the congregation calling him lies, that the proper steps may be taken for his regular settlement in that congregation: and the presbytery to which the congregation belongs, having received an authenticated certificate of his release, under the hand of the clerk of that presbytery, shall proceed to install him in the congregation, as soon as convenient. Provided always, that no bishop or pastor shall be translated without his own consent previously obtained.

IV. When any minister is to be settled in a congregation, the instalment, which consists in constituting a pastoral relation between him and the people of that particular church, may be performed either by the presbytery, or by a committee appointed for that purpose, as may appear most expedient: and the following order shall be observed therein:

V. A day shall be appointed for the instalment at such time as may appear most convenient, and due notice thereof given to the congregation.

VI. When the presbytery, or committee shall be convened and constituted, on the day appointed, a sermon shall be delivered by some one of the members previously appointed thereto; immediately after which, the bishop who is to preside shall state to the congregation the design of their meeting, and briefly recite the proceedings of the presbytery relative thereto. And then, addressing himself to the minister to be installed, shall propose to him the following or similar questions:

1. Are you now willing to take the charge of this congregation, as their pastor, agreeably to your declaration at accepting their call?

2. Do you conscientiously believe and declare, as far as you know your own heart, that in taking upon you this charge, you are influenced by a sincere desire to promote the glory of God, and the good of his church?

3. Do you solemnly promise, that, by the assistance of the grace of God, you will endeavour faithfully to discharge all the duties of a pastor to this congregation, and will be careful to maintain a deportment in all respects becoming a minister of the gospel of Christ, agreeably to your ordination engagements?

To all these having received satisfactory answers, he shall propose to the people the same or like questions as those directed under the head of ordination; which, having been also satisfactorily answered, by holding up the right hand in testimony of assent, he shall solemnly pronounce and declare the said minister to be regularly constituted the pastor of that congregation. A charge shall then be given to both parties, as directed in the case of ordination: and, after prayer, and singing a psalm adapted to the transaction, the congregation shall be dismissed with the usual benediction.

VII. It is highly becoming, that, after the solemnity of the instalment, the heads of families of that congregation who are then present, or at least the elders, and those appointed to take care of the temporal concerns of that church, should come forward to their pastor, and give him their right hand, in token of cordial reception and affectionate regard.

CHAPTER XVII.

OF RESIGNING A PASTORAL CHARGE.

WHEN any minister shall labour under such grievances in his congregation, as that he shall desire leave to resign his pastoral charge, the presbytery shall cite the congregation to appear, by their commissioners, at their next meeting, to show cause, if any they have, why the presbytery should not accept the resignation. If the congregation fail to appear, or if their reasons for retaining their pastor be deemed by the presbytery insufficient, he shall have leave granted to resign his pastoral charge, of which due record shall be made: and that church shall be held to be vacant, till supplied again, in an orderly manner, with another minister: and if any congregation shall desire to be released from their pastor, a similar process, *mutatis mutandis*, shall be observed.

CHAPTER XVIII.

OF MISSIONS.

WHEN vacancies become so numerous in any presbytery that they cannot be supplied with the frequent administration of the word and ordinances, it shall be proper for such presbytery, or any vacant congregation within their bounds, with the leave of the presbytery, to apply to any other presbytery, or to any synod, or to the General Assembly, for such assistance as they can afford. And, when any presbytery shall send any of their ministers or probationers to distant vacancies, the missionary shall be ready to produce his credentials to the presbytery or presbyteries, through the bounds of which he may pass, or at least to a committee thereof, and obtain their approbation. And the General Assembly may, of their own knowledge, send missions to any part to plant churches, or to supply vacancies: and, for this purpose, may direct any presbytery to ordain evangelists, or ministers without relation to particular churches: provided always, that such missions be made with the consent of the parties appointed; and that the judicatory sending them, make the necessary provision for their support and reward in the performance of this service.

CHAPTER XIX.

OF MODERATORS.

I. IT is equally necessary in the judicatories of the church, as in other assemblies that there should be a moderator or president; that the business may be conducted with order and despatch.

II. The moderator is to be considered as possessing, by delegation from the whole body, all authority necessary for the preservation of order; for convening and adjourning the judicatory; and directing its operations according to the rules of the church. He is to propose to the judicatory every subject of deliberation that comes before them. He may propose what appears to him the most regular and speedy way of bringing any business to issue. He shall prevent the members from interrupting each other; and require them, in speaking, always to address the chair. He shall prevent a speaker from deviating from the subject; and from using personal reflections. He shall silence those who refuse to obey order. He shall prevent members who attempt to leave the judicatory without leave obtained from him. He shall, at a proper season, when the deliberations are ended, put the question and call the votes. If the judicatory be equally divided, he shall possess the casting vote. If he be not willing to decide, he shall put the question a second time; and if the judicatory be again equally divided, and he decline to give his vote, the question shall be lost. In all questions he shall give a concise and clear state of the object of the vote; and the vote being taken, shall then declare how the question is decided. And he shall likewise be empowered, on any extraordinary emergency, to convene the judicatory, by his circular letter, before the ordinary time of meeting.

III. The moderator of the presbytery shall be chosen from year to year, or at every meeting of the presbytery, as the presbytery may think best. The moderator of the synod, and of the General Assembly, shall be chosen at each meeting of those judicatories: and the moderator, or, in case of his absence, another member appointed for the purpose, shall open the next meeting with a sermon, and shall hold the chair till a new moderator be chosen.

CHAPTER XX.

OF CLERKS.

EVERY judicatory shall choose a clerk, to record their transactions, whose continuance shall be during pleasure. It shall be the duty of the clerk, besides recording the transactions, to preserve the records carefully; and to grant extracts from them, whenever properly required: and such extracts, under the hand of the clerk, shall be considered as authentic vouchers of the fact which they declare, in any ecclesiastical judicatory, and to every part of the church.

CHAPTER XXI.

OF VACANT CONGREGATIONS ASSEMBLING FOR PUBLIC WORSHIP.

CONSIDERING the great importance of weekly assembling the people, for the public worship of God, in order thereby to improve their knowledge; to confirm their habits of worship, and their desire of the public ordinances; to augment their reverence for the most high God; and to promote the charitable affections which unite men most firmly in society: it is recommended, that every vacant congregation meet together, on the Lord's day, at one or more places, for the purpose of prayer, singing praises, and reading the holy Scriptures, together with the works of such approved divines, as the presbytery, within whose bounds they are, may recommend, and they may be able to procure; and that the elders or deacons be the persons who shall preside, and select the portions of Scripture, and of the other books to be read ; and to see that the whole be conducted in a becoming and orderly manner.

CHAPTER XXII.

OF COMMISSIONERS TO THE GENERAL ASSEMBLY.

I. THE commissioners to the General Assembly shall always be appointed by the presbytery from which they come, at its last stated meeting, immediately preceding the meeting of the General Assembly ; provided, that there be a sufficient interval between that time and the meeting of the Assembly, for the commissioners to attend to their duty in due season; otherwise, the presbytery may make the appointment at any stated meeting, not more than seven months preceding the meeting of the Assembly. And as much as possible to prevent all failure in the representation of the presbyteries, arising from unforeseen accidents to those first appointed, it may be expedient for each presbytery, in the room of each commissioner, to appoint also an alternate commissioner to supply his place, in case of necessary absence.

II. Each commissioner, before his name shall be enrolled as a member of the Assembly, shall produce from his presbytery, a commission under the hand of the moderator and clerk, in the following, or like form   viz.

" The presbytery of   being met at
"   on the   day of

"doth hereby appoint   bishop of the
"congregation of   [or
"ruling elder in the congregation of   as
"the case may be ;"] (to which the presbytery
may, if they think proper, make a substitution
in the following form) "or in case of his absence,
"then   bishop of the congregation of
"   [or   ruling elder in the con-
"gregation of   as the case may be :]
"to be a commissioner, on behalf of this presby-
"tery, to the next General Assembly of the
"Presbyterian Church in the United States of
"America, to meet at   on the
"day of   A. D.   or wherever,
"and whenever the said Assembly may happen
"to sit; to consult, vote, and determine, on all
"things that may come before that body, ac-
"cording to the principles and constitution of
"this church, and the word of God. And of
"his diligence herein, he is to render an ac-
"count at his return.
    Signed by order of the presbytery,
                    Moderator,
                    Clerk."
And the presbytery shall make record of the
appointment.
    III. In order, as far as possible, to procure
a respectable and full delegation to all our judicatories, it is proper that the expenses of
ministers and elders in their attendance on
these judicatories, be defrayed by the bodies
which they respectively represent.

BOOK II.

OF DISCIPLINE.

[AS RATIFIED BY THE GENERAL ASSEMBLY, 1884-85.]

CHAPTER I.

OF DISCIPLINE: ITS NATURE, ENDS AND SUBJECTS.

1. DISCIPLINE is the exercise of that authority, and the application of that system of laws, which the Lord Jesus Christ has appointed in his Church; embracing the care and control, maintained by the Church, over its members, officers and judicatories.

2. The ends of Discipline are the maintenance of the truth, the vindication of the authority and honor of Christ, the removal of offences, the promotion of the purity and edification of the Church, and the spiritual good of offenders. Its exercise, in such a manner as to secure its appropriate ends, requires much prudence and discretion. Judicatories, therefore, should take into consideration all the circumstances which may give a different character to conduct, and render it more or less offensive; and which may require different action, in similar cases, at different times, for the attainment of the same ends.

3. An offence is anything, in the doctrine, principles or practice of a church member, officer or judicatory, which is contrary to the Word of God; or which, if it be not in its own nature sinful, may tempt others to sin, or mar their spiritual edification.

4. Nothing shall, therefore, be the object of judicial process, which cannot be proved to be contrary to the Holy Scriptures, or to the regulations and practice of the Church founded thereon; nor anything which does not involve those evils which Discipline is intended to prevent.

5. All children born within the pale of the visible Church are members of the Church, are to be baptized, are under the care of the Church, and subject to its government and discipline, and when they have arrived at years of discretion, they are bound to perform all the duties of church members.

CHAPTER II.

OF THE PARTIES IN CASES OF PROCESS.

6. PROCESS against an alleged offender shall not be commenced unless some person undertakes to sustain the charge; or unless a judicatory finds it necessary for the ends of discipline to investigate the alleged offence.

7. An offence, gross in itself, may have

been committed in such circumstances, that plainly the offender cannot be prosecuted to conviction. In all such cases, it is better to wait until God, in his righteous providence, shall give further light, than, by unavailing prosecution, to weaken the force of discipline.

8. No prosecution shall be allowed in a case of alleged personal injury, where the injured party is the prosecutor, unless those means of reconciliation have been tried, which are required by our Lord, Matthew xviii. 15–17: "If thy brother shall trespass against thee, go and tell him his fault between thee and him alone; if he shall hear thee, thou hast gained thy brother. But if he will not hear thee, then take with thee one or two more, that in the mouth of two or three witnesses every word may be established. And if he shall neglect to hear them, tell it unto the Church."

9. The course prescribed by the preceding section shall not be required when the prosecution is initiated by a judicatory; but in all such cases, and in every case of prosecution by a private person other than the injured party, effort should be made, by private conference with the accused, to avoid, if possible, the necessity of actual process.

10. When the prosecution is initiated by a judicatory, THE PRESBYTERIAN CHURCH IN THE UNITED STATES OF AMERICA shall be the prosecutor, and an original party; in all

other cases, the individual prosecutor shall be an original party.

11. When the prosecution is initiated by a judicatory, it shall appoint one or more of its own members a Committee to conduct the prosecution in all its stages in whatever judicatory, until the final issue be reached: *provided*, that any appellate judicatory before which the case is pending shall, if desired by the prosecuting committee, appoint one or more of its own members to assist in the prosecution, upon the nomination of the prosecuting committee.

12. If one, who considers himself slandered, requests an investigation which a judicatory finds it proper to institute, one or more of its members shall be appointed to investigate the alleged slander, and make report in writing: and a record thereafter made may conclude the matter.

13. Great caution ought to be exercised in receiving accusations from any person who is known to indulge a malignant spirit toward the accused, or who is not of good character, or who is himself under censure or process, or who is personally interested in any respect in the conviction of the accused, or who is known to be litigious, rash or highly imprudent.

14. Any person who appears as a prosecutor, without appointment by the judicatory, shall be warned before the charges are pre-

sented that, if he fail to show probable cause for the charges, he must himself be censured, as a slanderer of the brethren, in proportion to the malignancy or rashness which may appear in the prosecution.

CHAPTER III.

OF CHARGES AND SPECIFICATIONS.

15. THE charge shall set forth the alleged offence; and the specifications shall set forth the facts relied upon to sustain the charge. Each specification shall declare, as far as possible, the time, place, and circumstances, and shall be accompanied with the names of the witnesses to be cited for its support.

16. A charge shall not allege more than one offence; several charges against the same person, however, with the specifications under each of them, may be presented to the judicatory at one and the same time, and may, in the discretion of the judicatory, be tried together. But, when several charges are tried at the same time, a vote on each charge must be separately taken.

17. In all cases of alleged personal injury, where the prosecution is by the injured person or persons, the charge must be accompanied by an averment, that the course prescribed by our Lord, Matt. xviii. 15--17, has been faithfully tried.

CHAPTER IV.

OF PROCESS: GENERAL RULES PERTAINING TO ALL CASES.

18. ORIGINAL jurisdiction, in relation to Ministers, pertains to the Presbytery; in relation to others, to the Session. But the higher judicatories may institute process in cases in which the lower have been directed so to do, and have refused or neglected to obey.

19. When a judicatory enters on the consideration of an alleged offence, the charge and specifications, which shall be in writing, shall be read; and nothing more shall be done at that meeting, unless by consent of parties, than to furnish the accused with a copy of the charge and specifications, together with the names of all the witnesses then known to support each specification; and to cite all concerned to appear at a subsequent meeting of the judicatory, to be held not less than ten days after the service of the citations. The citations shall be signed, in the name of the judicatory, by the Moderator, or Clerk; who shall, also, furnish citations for such witnesses as either party shall name. The accused shall not be required to disclose the names of his witnesses.

20. Citations shall be served personally, unless the person to be cited cannot be found, in which case the citation shall be sent to his

last known place of residence; and, before proceeding to trial, it must appear that the citations have been served.

21. If an accused person refuses to obey a citation, a second citation shall issue, accompanied by a notice that, if he do not appear at the time appointed, unless providentially hindered, he will be censured for his contumacy, according to the subsequent provisions of the Book of Discipline. (*See Sections* 33, 38 *and* 46.) If he does not then appear, the judicatory may proceed to trial and judgment in his absence; in which case it shall appoint some person to represent him as counsel. The time allowed for his appearance, on any citation subsequent to the first, shall be determined by the judicatory, with proper regard for all the circumstances. The same rule, as to the time allowed for appearance, shall apply to all witnesses cited at the request of either party.

22. At the meeting at which the citations are returnable, the accused shall appear, or, if unable to be present, may appear by counsel. He may file objections to the regularity of the organization, or to the jurisdiction of the judicatory, or to the sufficiency of the charges and specifications in form or in legal effect, or any other substantial objection affecting the order or regularity of the proceeding, on which objections the parties shall be heard. The judicatory upon the filing such objections

shall, or on its own motion may, determine all such preliminary objections, and may dismiss the case, or permit, in the furtherance of justice, amendments to the specifications or charges not changing the general nature of the same. If the proceedings be found in order, and the charges and specifications be considered sufficient to put the accused on his defence, he shall plead "guilty," or "not guilty," to the same, which shall be entered on the record. If the plea be "guilty," the judicatory shall proceed to judgment; but if the plea be "not guilty," or if the accused decline to answer, a plea of "not guilty" shall be entered of record and the trial proceed.

23. The witnesses shall be examined, and, if desired, cross-examined, and any other competent evidence introduced, at a meeting of which the accused shall be properly notified; after which new witnesses and other evidence, in rebuttal only, may be introduced by either party. But evidence, discovered during the progress of the trial, may be admitted, in behalf of either party, under such regulations, as to notice of the names of witnesses and the nature of the proof, as the judicatory shall deem reasonable and proper; and then the parties themselves shall be heard. The judicatory shall then go into private session—the parties, their counsel and all other persons not members of the body being excluded; when, after careful deliberation, the judicatory

shall proceed to vote on each specification and on each charge separately, and judgment shall be entered accordingly.

24. The charge and specifications, the plea and the judgment, shall be entered on the minutes of the judicatory. The minutes shall also exhibit all the acts and orders of the judicatory relating to the case, with the reasons therefor, together with the notice of appeal, and the reasons therefor, if any shall have been filed; all which, together with the evidence in the case duly filed and authenticated by the Clerk of the judicatory, shall constitute the record of the case; and, in case of a removal thereof by appeal, the lower judicatory shall transmit the record to the higher. Nothing which is not contained in the record shall be taken into consideration in the higher judicatory.

25. Exceptions may be taken by either of the original parties in a trial, to any part of the proceedings, except in the judicatory of last resort, and shall be entered on the record.

26. No professional counsel shall be permitted to appear and plead in cases of process in any of our ecclesiastical judicatories. But if any accused person feel unable to represent and plead his own cause to advantage, he may request any minister or elder, belonging to the judicatory before which he appears, to prepare and exhibit his cause as he may judge proper. But the minister or elder so engaged

shall not be allowed, after pleading the cause of the accused, to sit in judgment as a member of the judicatory.

27. Questions as to order or evidence, arising in the course of a trial, shall, after the parties have had an opportunity to be heard, be decided by the Moderator, subject to appeal; and the question on the appeal shall be determined without debate. All such decisions, if desired by either party, shall be entered upon the record of the case.

28. No member of a judicatory, who has not been present during the whole of a trial, shall be allowed to vote on any question arising therein, except by unanimous consent of the judicatory and of the parties; and, when a trial is in progress, except in an appellate judicatory, the roll shall be called after each recess and adjournment, and the names of the absentees shall be noted.

29. The parties shall be allowed copies of the record at their own expense; and, on the final disposition of a case in a higher judicatory, the record of the case, with the judgment, shall be transmitted to the judicatory in which the case originated.

30. In the infliction and removal of church censures, judicatories shall observe the modes prescribed in Chapter X. of the Directory for Worship.

31. In all cases of judicial process, the judicatory may, at any stage of the case, deter-

mine, by a vote of two-thirds, to sit with closed doors.

32. A judicatory may, if the edification of the Church demands it, require an accused person to refrain from approaching the Lord's Table, or from the exercise of office, or both, until final action in the case shall be taken: *provided*, that in all cases a speedy investigation or trial shall be had.

CHAPTER V.

SPECIAL RULES PERTAINING TO CASES BEFORE SESSIONS.

33. WHEN an accused person has been twice duly cited, and refuses to appear, by himself or counsel, before a Session, or, appearing, refuses to answer the charge brought against him, he shall be suspended, by act of Session, from the communion of the Church, and shall so remain until he repents of his contumacy, and submits himself to the orders of the judicatory.

34. The censures to be inflicted by the Session are, Admonition, Rebuke, Suspension or Deposition from office, Suspension from the communion of the Church, and, in the case of offenders who will not be reclaimed by milder measures, Excommunication.

35. The sentence shall be published, if at

all, only in the Church or Churches which have been offended.

CHAPTER VI.

GENERAL RULES PERTAINING TO THE TRIAL OF A MINISTER, ELDER, OR DEACON.

36. As the honor and success of the gospel depend, in a great measure, on the character of its Ministers, each Presbytery ought, with the greatest care and impartiality, to watch over their personal and professional conduct. But as, on the one hand, no Minister ought, on account of his office, to be screened from the hand of justice, or his offences to be slightly censured, so neither ought charges to be received against him on slight grounds.

37. If a Minister be accused of an offence, at such a distance from his usual place of residence as that it is not likely to become otherwise known to his Presbytery, it shall be the duty of the Presbytery within whose bounds the offence is alleged to have been committed, if it shall be satisfied that there is probable ground for the accusation, to notify his Presbytery thereof, and of the nature of the offence; and his Presbytery, on receiving such notice, shall, if it appears that the honor of religion requires it, proceed to the trial of the case.

38. If a Minister accused of an offence re-

fuses to appear by himself or counsel, after being twice duly cited, he shall, for his contumacy, be suspended from his office; and if, after another citation, he refuses to appear by himself or counsel, he shall be suspended from the communion of the Church.

39. If a judicatory so decides, a member shall not be allowed, while charges are pending against him, to deliberate or vote on any question.

40. If the accused be found guilty, he shall be admonished, rebuked, suspended or deposed from office (with or without suspension from church privileges, in either case), or excommunicated. A Minister, suspended from office, may, at the expiration of one year, unless he gives satisfactory evidence of repentance, be deposed without further trial.

41. Heresy and schism may be of such a nature as to call for deposition; but errors ought to be carefully considered, whether they strike at the vitals of religion and are industriously spread, or whether they arise from the weakness of the human understanding, and are not likely to do much injury.

42. If the Presbytery finds, on trial, that the matter complained of amounts to no more than such acts of infirmity as may be amended and the people satisfied, so that little or nothing remains to hinder the usefulness of the offender, it shall take all prudent measures to remove the evil.

43. A Minister deposed for immoral conduct shall not be restored, even on the deepest sorrow for his sin, until after some considerable time of eminent and exemplary, humble and edifying conduct; and he ought in no case to be restored, until it shall clearly appear to the judicatory, within whose bounds he resides, that the restoration can be effected without injury to the cause of religion; and then only by the judicatory inflicting the censure, or with its advice and consent.

44. If a Minister is deposed without excommunication, his pulpit, if he is a Pastor, shall be declared vacant; and the Presbytery shall give him a letter to any church with which he may desire to connect himself where his lot may be cast, in which shall be stated his exact relation to the Church. If a Pastor is suspended from office only, the Presbytery may, if no appeal from the sentence of suspension is pending, declare his pulpit vacant.

45. A Presbytery may, if the edification of the Church demand it, require an accused Minister to refrain from the exercise of his office until final action in the case shall be taken: *provided*, that in all cases a speedy investigation or trial shall be had.

46. In process by a Session against a ruling elder or a deacon, the provisions of this chapter, so far as applicable, shall be observed.

CHAPTER VII.

OF CASES WITHOUT PROCESS.

47. If a person commits an offence in the presence of a judicatory, or comes forward as his own accuser and makes known his offence, the judicatory may proceed to judgment without process, giving the offender an opportunity to be heard; and in the case first named he may demand a delay of at least two days before judgment. The record must show the nature of the offence, as well as the judgment and the reasons therefor, and appeal may be taken from the judgment as in other cases.

48. If a communicant, not chargeable with immoral conduct, inform the Session that he is fully persuaded that he has no right to come to the Lord's Table, the Session shall confer with him on the subject, and may, should he continue of the same mind, and his attendance on the other means of grace be regular, excuse him from attendance on the Lord's Supper; and, after fully satisfying themselves that his judgment is not the result of mistaken views, shall erase his name from the roll of communicants, and make record of their action in the case.

49. If a communicant, not chargeable with immoral conduct, removes out of the bounds of his Church, without asking for or receiving a regular certificate of dismission to another Church, and his residence is known, the

Session may, within two years, advise him to apply for such certificate; and, if he fails so to do, without giving sufficient reason, his name may be placed on the roll of suspended members, until he shall satisfy the Session of the propriety of his restoration. But, if the Session has no knowledge of him for the space of three years, it may erase his name from the roll of communicants, making record of its action and the reasons therefor. In either case, the member shall continue subject to the jurisdiction of the Session. A separate roll of all such names shall be kept, stating the relations of each to the Church.

50. If any communicant, not chargeable with immoral conduct, neglects the ordinances of the Church for one year, and in circumstances such as the Session shall regard to be a serious injury to the cause of religion, he may, after affectionate visitation by the Session, and admonition if need be, be suspended from the communion of the Church until he gives satisfactory evidence of the sincerity of his repentance, but he shall not be excommunicated without due process of discipline.

51. If a Minister, otherwise in good standing, shall make application to be released from the office of the ministry, he may, at the discretion of the Presbytery, be put on probation, for one year at least, in such a manner as the Presbytery may direct, in order to ascertain his motives and reasons for such a re-

linquishment. And if, at the end of this period, the Presbytery be satisfied that he cannot be useful and happy in the exercise of his ministry, they may allow him to demit the office, and return to the condition of a private member in the Church, ordering his name to be stricken from the roll of the Presbytery, and giving him a letter to any Church with which he may desire to connect himself.

52. If a communicant renounces the communion of this Church by joining another denomination, without a regular dismission, although such conduct is disorderly, the Session shall take no other action in the case than to record the fact, and order his name to be erased from the roll. If charges are pending against him, these charges may be prosecuted.

53. If a Minister, not otherwise chargeable with an offence, renounces the jurisdiction of this Church, by abandoning the ministry, or becoming independent, or joining another denomination not deemed heretical, without a regular dismission, the Presbytery shall take no other action than to record the fact and to erase his name from the roll. If charges are pending against him, he may be tried thereon. If it appears that he has joined another denomination deemed heretical, he may be suspended, deposed, or excommunicated.

CHAPTER VIII.

OF EVIDENCE.

54. JUDICATORIES ought to be very careful and impartial in receiving testimony. Not every person is competent, and not every competent person is credible, as a witness.

55. All persons, whether parties or otherwise, are competent witnesses, except such as do not believe in the existence of God, or a future state of rewards and punishments, or have not sufficient intelligence to understand the obligation of an oath. Any witness may be challenged for incompetency, and the judicatory shall decide the question.

56. The credibility of a witness, or the degree of credit due to his testimony, may be affected by relationship to any of the parties; by interest in the result of the trial; by want of proper age; by weakness of understanding; by infamy or malignity of character; by being under church censure; by general rashness or indiscretion; or by any other circumstances that appear to affect his veracity, knowledge or interest in the case.

57. A husband or wife shall be a competent witness for or against the other, but shall not be compelled to testify.

58. Evidence may be oral, written or printed, direct or circumstantial. A charge may be proven by the testimony of one witness, only when supported by other evidence; but,

when there are several specifications under the same general charge, the proof of two or more of the specifications, by different credible witnesses, shall be sufficient to establish the charge.

59. No witness, afterwards to be examined, except a member of the judicatory, shall be present during the examination of another witness if either party object.

60. Witnesses shall be examined first by the party producing them; then cross-examined by the opposite party; after which any member of the judicatory or either party may put additional interrogatories. Irrelevant or frivolous questions shall not be admitted, nor leading questions by the parties producing the witness, except under permission of the judicatory as necessary to elicit the truth.

61. The oath or affirmation shall be administered by the Moderator in the following, or like, terms: "You solemnly promise, in the presence of the omniscient and heart-searching God, that you will declare the truth, the whole truth, and nothing but the truth, according to the best of your knowledge, in the matter in which you are called to testify, as you shall answer to the Great Judge of quick and dead."

62. Every question put to a witness shall, if required, be reduced to writing. And, if either party desire it, or if the judicatory shall

so decide, both question and answer shall be recorded. The testimony, thus recorded, shall be read to the witnesses, in the presence of the judicatory, for their approbation and subscription.

63. The records of a judicatory, or any part of them, whether original or transcribed, if regularly authenticated by the Clerk, or in case of his death, absence, disability or failure from any cause, by the Moderator, shall be deemed good and sufficient evidence in every other judicatory.

64. In like manner, testimony taken by one judicatory, and regularly certified, shall be received by every other judicatory, as no less valid than if it had been taken by themselves.

65. Any judicatory, before which a case may be pending, shall have power, whenever the necessity of parties or witnesses shall require it, to appoint, on the application of either party, a Commission of Ministers, or Elders, or both, to examine witnesses; which Commission, if the case requires it, may be of persons within the jurisdiction of another body. The Commissioners so appointed shall take such testimony as may be offered by either party. The testimony shall be taken in accordance with the rules governing the judicatory, either orally or on written interrogatories and cross-interrogatories, duly settled by the judicatory, due notice having been

given of the time when, and place where, the witnesses are to be examined. All questions, as to the relevancy or competency of the testimony so taken, shall be determined by the judicatory. The testimony, properly authenticated by the signatures of the Commissioners, shall be transmitted, in due time, to the Clerk of the judicatory before which the case is pending.

66. A member of the judicatory may be called upon to testify in a case which comes before it. He shall be qualified as other witnesses are, and, after having given his testimony, may immediately resume his seat as a member of the judicatory.

67. A member of the Church, summoned as a witness, and refusing to appear, or, having appeared, refusing to testify, shall be censured according to the circumstances of the case for his contumacy.

68. If, after a trial before any judicatory, new evidence is discovered, supposed to be important to the exculpation of the accused, he may ask, if the case has not been appealed, and the judicatory shall grant, if justice seems to require it, a new trial.

69. If, in the prosecution of an appeal, new evidence is offered, which, in the judgment of the appellate judicatory, has an important bearing on the case, it shall either refer the whole case to the inferior judicatory for a new trial; or, with the consent of the

DISCIPLINE. 481

parties, take the testimony, and hear and determine the case.

CHAPTER IX.

OF THE WAYS IN WHICH A CAUSE MAY BE CARRIED FROM A LOWER TO A HIGHER JUDICATORY.

70. ALL proceedings of the Session, the Presbytery, and the Synod (except as limited by Chapter XI., Section 4, of the Form of Government), are subject to review by, and may be taken to, a superior judicatory, by General Review and Control, Reference, Complaint or Appeal.

I. OF GENERAL REVIEW AND CONTROL.

71. All proceedings of the Church shall be reported to, and reviewed by, the Session, and by its order incorporated with its Records. Every judicatory above a Session shall review, at least once a year, the records of the proceedings of the judicatory next below; and, if the lower judicatory shall omit to send up its records for this purpose, the higher may require them to be produced, either immediately, or at a specified time, as circumstances may determine.

72. In such review, the judicatory shall examine, first, whether the proceedings have been correctly recorded; second, whether they

have been constitutional and regular; and third, whether they have been wise, equitable and for the edification of the Church.

73. Members of a judicatory, the records of which are under review, shall not be allowed to vote thereon.

74. In most cases the superior judicatory may discharge its duty, by simply placing on its own records, and on those under review, the censure which it may pass. But irregular proceedings may be found so disreputable and injurious, that the inferior judicatory must be required to review and correct, or reverse them, and report, within a specified time, its obedience to the order: *provided*, however, that no judicial decision shall be reversed, unless regularly taken up by appeal or complaint.

75. If a judicatory is, at any time, well advised of any unconstitutional proceedings of a lower judicatory, the latter shall be cited to appear, at a specified time and place, to produce the records, and to show what it has done in the matter in question; after which, if the charge is sustained, the whole matter shall be concluded by the judicatory itself, or be remitted to the lower judicatory, with direction as to its disposition.

76. Judicatories may sometimes neglect to perform their duty, by which neglect heretical opinions or corrupt practices may be allowed to gain ground, or offenders of a gross

character may be suffered to escape; or some part of their proceedings may have been omitted from the record, or not properly recorded. If, therefore, at any time, the superior judicatory is well advised of such neglects, omissions, or irregularities on the part of the inferior judicatory, it may require its records to be produced, and shall either proceed to examine and decide the whole matter, as completely as if proper record had been made; or it shall cite the lower judicatory, and proceed as in the next preceding section.

II. OF REFERENCES.

77. A Reference is a representation in writing, made by an inferior to a superior judicatory, of a judicial case not yet decided. Generally, however, it is more conducive to the public good that each judicatory should fulfil its duty by exercising its own judgment.

78. Cases which are new, important, difficult, or of peculiar delicacy, the decision of which may establish principles or precedents of extensive influence, on which the inferior judicatory is greatly divided, or on which for any reason it is desirable that a superior judicatory should first decide, are proper subjects of Reference.

79. References are, either for mere advice, preparatory to a decision by the inferior judicatory, or for ultimate trial and decision by

the superior; and are to be carried to the next higher judicatory. If for advice, the Reference only suspends the decision of the inferior judicatory; if for trial, it submits the whole case to the final judgment of the superior.

80. In cases of Reference, members of the inferior judicatory may sit, deliberate, and vote.

81. A judicatory is not necessarily bound to give a final judgment in a case of Reference, but may remit the whole case, either with or without advice, to the inferior judicatory.

82. The whole record of proceedings shall be promptly transmitted to the superior judicatory, and, if the Reference is accepted, the parties shall be heard.

III. OF COMPLAINTS.

83. A Complaint is a written representation, made to the next superior judicatory, by one or more persons subject and submitting to the jurisdiction of the judicatory complained of, respecting any delinquency, or any decision, by an inferior judicatory.

84. Written notice of Complaint, with the reasons therefor, shall be given, within ten days after the action was taken, to the Clerk, or, in case of his death, absence, or disability, to the Moderator, of the judicatory complained of, who shall lodge it, with the records and all the papers pertaining to the case, with the Clerk of the superior judicatory, be-

fore the close of the second day of its regular meeting next ensuing the date of the reception of said notice.

85. Whenever a Complaint, in cases nonjudicial, is entered against a decision of a judicatory, signed by at least one-third of the members recorded as present when the action was taken, the execution of such decision shall be stayed, until the final issue of the case by the superior judicatory.

86. The complainant shall lodge his Complaint, and the reasons therefor, with the Clerk of the superior judicatory before the close of the second day of its meeting next ensuing the date of the notice thereof.

87. If the higher judicatory finds that the Complaint is in order, and that sufficient reasons for proceeding to trial have been assigned, the next step shall be to read the record of the action complained of, and so much of the record of the lower judicatory as may be pertinent; then the parties shall be heard, and, after that, the judicatory shall proceed to consider and determine the case, as provided for in cases of original process. In cases of Complaint involving a judicial decision, proceedings in an appellate judicatory shall be had in the order and as provided in Section 99, Chapter IV., entitled "Of Appeals."

88. The effect of a Complaint, if sustained, may be the reversal, in whole or in part, of the action of the lower judicatory; and may

also, in cases non-judicial, be the infliction of censure upon the judicatory complained of. When a Complaint is sustained, the lower judicatory shall be directed how to dispose of the matter.

89. The parties to a Complaint, in cases non-judicial, shall be known, respectively, as Complainant and Respondent—the latter being the judicatory complained of, which should always be represented by one or more of its number appointed for that purpose, who may be assisted by counsel.

90. Neither the Complainant nor the members of the judicatory complained of shall sit, deliberate, or vote in the case.

91. Either of the parties to a Complaint may appeal to the next superior judicatory, except as limited by Chapter XI., Section 4, of the Form of Government.

92. The judicatory against which a Complaint is made shall send up its records, and all the papers relating to the matter of the Complaint, and filed with the record; and, for failure to do this, it shall be censured by the superior judicatory, which shall have power to make such orders, pending the production of the records and papers, and the determination of the Complaint, as may be necessary to preserve the rights of all the parties.

93. If a case should be carried to an appellate judicatory by both Appeal and Complaint, the same shall be consolidated for trial,

if deemed proper by the appellate judicatory.
If the Appeal be abandoned, the case shall be
heard only on the Complaint.

IV. OF APPEALS.

94. An Appeal is the removal of a judicial
case, by a written representation, from an inferior to a superior judicatory; and may be
taken, by either of the original parties, from
the final judgment of the lower judicatory.
These parties shall be called Appellant and
Appellee.

95. The grounds of Appeal may be such
as these: Irregularity in the proceedings of
the inferior judicatory; refusal to entertain
an Appeal or Complaint; refusal of reasonable indulgence to a party on trial; receiving
improper, or declining to receive important,
testimony; hastening to a decision before the
testimony is fully taken; manifestation of
prejudice in the conduct of the case; and mistake or injustice in the decision.

96. Written notice of Appeal, with specifications of the errors alleged, shall be given,
within ten days after the judgment has been
rendered, to the Clerk, or, in case of his death,
absence, or disability, to the Moderator, of the
judicatory appealed from, who shall lodge it,
with the records and all the papers pertaining
to the case, with the Clerk of the superior
judicatory, before the close of the second day

of its regular meeting next ensuing the date of his reception of said notice.

97. The appellant shall appear in person or by counsel before the judicatory appealed to, on or before the close of the second day of its regular meeting next ensuing the date of the filing of his notice of Appeal, and shall lodge his Appeal and specifications of the errors alleged, with the Clerk of the superior judicatory, within the time above specified. If he fail to show to the satisfaction of the judicatory that he was unavoidably prevented from so doing, he shall be considered as having abandoned his Appeal, and the judgment shall stand.

98. Neither the appellant, nor the members of the judicatory appealed from, shall sit, deliberate, or vote in the case.

99. When due notice of an Appeal has been given, and the Appeal and the specifications of the errors alleged have been filed in due time, the Appeal shall be considered in order. The judgment, the notice of Appeal, the Appeal, and the specifications of the errors alleged, shall be read; and the judicatory may then determine, after hearing the parties, whether the Appeal shall be entertained. If it be entertained, the following order shall be observed:

(1) The record in the case, from the beginning, shall be read, except what may be omitted by consent.

(2) The parties shall be heard, the appellant opening and closing.

(3) Opportunity shall be given to the members of the judicatory appealed from to be heard.

(4) Opportunity shall be given to the members of the superior judicatory to be heard.

(5) The vote shall then be separately taken, without debate, on each specification of error alleged, the question being taken in the form: "Shall the specification of error be sustained?" If no one of the specifications be sustained, and no error be found by the judicatory in the record, the judgment of the inferior judicatory shall be affirmed. If one or more errors be found, the judicatory shall determine, whether the judgment of the inferior judicatory shall be reversed or modified, or the case remanded for a new trial; and the judgment, accompanied by a recital of the error or errors found, shall be entered on the record. If the judicatory deem it wise, an explanatory minute may be adopted which shall be a part of the record of the case.

100. When the judgment directs admonition or rebuke, notice of Appeal shall suspend all further proceedings; but in other cases the judgments shall be in force until the Appeal is decided.

101. The judicatory whose judgment is appealed from shall send up its records, and all the papers relating thereto, and filed with

the record. If it fails to do this, it shall be censured; and the sentence appealed from shall be suspended, until a record is produced on which the issue can be fairly tried.

102. Appeals are, generally, to be taken to the judicatory immediately superior to that appealed from.

CHAPTER X.

OF DISSENTS AND PROTESTS.

103. A Dissent is a declaration of one or more members of a minority in a judicatory, expressing disagreement with a decision of the majority in a particular case.

104. A Protest is a more formal declaration, made by one or more members of a minority, bearing testimony against what is deemed a mischievous or erroneous proceeding, decision or judgment, and including a statement of the reasons therefor.

105. If a Dissent or Protest be couched in decorous and respectful language, and be without offensive reflections or insinuations against the majority, it shall be entered on the records.

106. The judicatory may prepare an answer to any protest which imputes to it principles or reasonings which its action does not import, and the answer shall also be entered upon the records. Leave may thereupon be

given to the protestant or protestants, if they desire it, to modify their Protest; and the answer of the judicatory may also, in consequence, be modified. This shall end the matter.

107. No one shall be allowed to dissent or protest who has not a right to vote on the question decided,—and, in judicial cases, no one shall be allowed to dissent or protest who did not vote against the decision.

CHAPTER XI.

OF JURISDICTION IN CASES OF DISMISSION.

108. THE judicatory, to which a church member or a Minister belongs, shall have sole jurisdiction for the trial of offences whenever or wherever committed by him.

109. A member of a Church, receiving a certificate of dismission to another Church, shall continue to be a member of the Church giving him the certificate, and subject to the jurisdiction of its Session (but shall not deliberate or vote in a church meeting, nor exercise the functions of any office), until he has become a member of the Church to which he is recommended, or some other evangelical Church; and, should he return the certificate, within a year from its date, the Session shall make record of the fact, but he shall not thereby be restored to the exercise of the

functions of any office previously held by him in that Church.

110. In like manner, a Minister shall be subject to the jurisdiction of the Presbytery which dismissed him (but shall not deliberate or vote, nor be counted in the basis of representation to the General Assembly), until he actually becomes a member of another Presbytery; but, should he return the certificate of dismission within a year from its date, the Presbytery shall make record of the fact, and restore him to the full privileges of membership.

111. A Presbytery, giving a certificate of dismission to a Minister, Licentiate, or Candidate for licensure, shall specify the particular body to which he is recommended; and, if recommended to a Presbytery, no other than the one designated, if existing, shall receive him.

112. If a Church becomes extinct, the Presbytery with which it was connected shall have jurisdiction over its members, and grant them letters of dismission to some other Church. It shall, also, determine any case of discipline begun by the Session and not concluded.

113. If a Presbytery becomes extinct, the Synod, with which it was connected, shall have jurisdiction over its members, and may transfer them to any Presbytery within its bounds. It shall, also, determine any case of discipline begun by the Presbytery and not concluded.

CHAPTER XII.

OF REMOVALS, AND LIMITATION OF TIME.

114. When any member shall remove from one Church to another, he shall produce a certificate, ordinarily not more than one year old, of his church-membership and dismission, before he shall be admitted as a regular member of that Church.

The names of the baptized children of a parent seeking dismission to another Church shall, if such children are members of his household and remove with him and are not themselves communicants, be included in the certificate of dismission. The certificate shall be addressed to a particular Church, and the fact of the reception of the person or persons named in it shall be promptly communicated to the Church which gave it.

115. In like manner, when a Minister, Licentiate, or Candidate, is dismissed from one Presbytery to another, the certificate shall be presented to the Presbytery, to which it is addressed, ordinarily within one year from its date, and the fact of his reception shall be promptly communicated to the Presbytery dismissing him.

116. If a church-member, more than two years absent from the place of his ordinary residence and Church connections, applies for a certificate of membership, his absence, and

the knowledge of the Church respecting his demeanor for that time, or its want of information concerning it, shall be distinctly stated in the certificate.

117. Prosecution for an alleged offence shall commence within one year from the time of its alleged commission, or from the date when it becomes known to the judicatory which has jurisdiction thereof.

CHAPTER XIII.

JUDICIAL COMMISSIONS.

118. The General Assembly, and each Synod under its care, shall have power to appoint a Judicial Commission from their respective bodies, consisting of ministers and elders, in number not less than a quorum of the judicatory appointing.

All judicial cases may be submitted to this Commission, and its decisions shall be final, except in matters of law, which shall be referred to the appointing court for final adjudication; and also all matters of Constitution and Doctrine, which may be reviewed in the appointing body, and upon final adjudication by the General Assembly. The Commission shall sit at the same time and place as the body appointing it, and its findings shall be entered upon the minutes of such body.

THE
DIRECTORY
FOR THE
WORSHIP OF GOD IN THE PRESBYTERIAN CHURCH
IN THE UNITED STATES OF AMERICA,*

AS AMENDED AND RATIFIED BY THE GENERAL ASSEMBLY,

In May, 1821.

CHAPTER I.
OF THE SANCTIFICATION OF THE LORD'S DAY.

I. IT is the duty of every person to remember the Lord's day; and to prepare for it, before its approach. All worldly business should be so ordered, and seasonably laid aside, as that we may not be hindered thereby from sanctifying the Sabbath, as the Holy Scriptures require.

II. The whole day is to be kept wholly to the Lord; and to be employed in the public and private exercises of religion. Therefore, it is requisite, that there be a holy resting, all the day, from unnecessary labours; and an abstaining from those recreations which may

---

* The Scripture-warrant for what is specified in the various articles of this directory, will be found at large in the Confession of Faith and Catechisms, in the places where the subjects a e treated in a doctrinal form.

be lawful on other days; and also, as much as possible, from worldly thoughts and conversation.

III. Let the provisions for the support of the family on that day, be so ordered, that servants or others be not improperly detained from the public worship of God; nor hindered from sanctifying the Sabbath.

IV. Let every person and family, in the morning, by secret and private prayer, for themselves and others, especially for the assistance of God to their minister, and for a blessing upon his ministry, by reading the Scriptures, and by holy meditation, prepare for communion with God in his public ordinances.

V. Let the people be careful to assemble at the appointed time; that, being all present at the beginning, they may unite, with one heart, in all the parts of public worship: and let none unnecessarily depart, till after the blessing be pronounced.

VI. Let the time after the solemn services of the congregation in public are over, be spent in reading, meditation, repeating of sermons, catechizing, religious conversation, prayer for a blessing upon the public ordinances, the singing of psalms, hymns, or spiritual songs;—visiting the sick, relieving the poor, and in performing such like duties of piety, charity, and mercy.

CHAPTER II.

)F THE ASSEMBLING OF THE CONGREGATION AND THEIR BEHAVIOUR DURING DIVINE SERVICE.

I. WHEN the time appointed for public worship is come, let the people enter the church, and take their seats in a decent, grave, and reverent manner.

II. In time of public worship, let all the people attend with gravity and reverence; forbearing to read any thing, except what the minister is then reading or citing; abstaining from all whisperings, from salutations of persons present, or coming in; and from gazing about, sleeping, smiling, and all other indecent behaviour.

CHAPTER III.

OF THE PUBLIC READING OF THE HOLY SCRIPTURES.

I. THE reading of the Holy Scriptures, in the congregation, is a part of the public worship of God, and ought to be performed by the ministers and teachers.

II. The Holy Scriptures of the Old and New Testament, shall be publicly read, from the most approved translation, in the vulgar tongue, that all may hear and understand.

III. How large a portion shall be read at

once, is left to the discretion of every minister: however, in each service, he ought to read, at least, one chapter; and more, when the chapters are short, or the connection requires it. He may, when he thinks it expedient, expound any part of what is read: always having regard to the time, that neither reading, singing, praying, preaching, or any other ordinance, be disproportionate the one to the other; nor the whole rendered too short, or too tedious.

CHAPTER IV.

OF THE SINGING OF PSALMS.

I. It is the duty of Christians to praise God, by singing psalms, or hymns, publicly in the church, as also privately in the family.

II. In singing the praises of God, we are to sing with the spirit, and with the understanding also; making melody in our hearts unto the Lord. It is also proper, that we cultivate some knowledge of the rules of music; that we may praise God in a becoming manner with our voices, as well as with our hearts.

III. The whole congregation should be furnished with books, and ought to join in this part of worship. It is proper to sing without parcelling out the psalm, line by line. The practice of reading the psalm, line by line, was introduced in times of ignorance, when many in the congregation could not read: therefore, it is recommended, that it be laid aside, as far as convenient.

IV. The proportion of the time of public worship to be spent in singing, is left to the prudence of every minister: but it is recommended, that more time be allowed for this excellent part of divine service than has been usual in most of our churches.

CHAPTER V.

OF PUBLIC PRAYER.

1. It seems very proper to begin the public worship of the sanctuary by a short prayer; humbly adoring the infinite majesty of the living God; expressing a sense of our distance from him as creatures, and unworthiness as sinners; and humbly imploring his gracious presence, the assistance of his Holy Spirit in the duties of his worship, and his acceptance of us through the merits of our Lord and Saviour Jesus Christ.

II. Then, after singing a psalm, or hymn, it is proper that, before sermon, there should be a full and comprehensive prayer: *First,* Adoring the glory and perfections of God, as they are made known to us in the works of creation, in the conduct of providence, and in the clear and full revelation he hath made of himself in his written word: *Second,* Giving thanks to him for all his mercies of every kind, general and particular, spiritual and temporal, common and special; above all, for Christ Jesus, his unspeakable gift, and the hope of eternal life through him : *Third*, Making humble confession of sin, both original and actual ; acknowledging, and endeavouring to impress the mind of every worshipper, with a deep sense of the evil of all sin, as such ; as being a departure from the living God ; and also taking a particular and affecting view of the various fruits which proceed from this root of bitterness:— as sins against God, our neighbour and ourselves ; sins in thought, in word, and in deed ; sins secret and presumptuous ; sins accidental and habitual. Also, the aggravations of sin, arising from knowledge, or the means of it ; from distinguishing mercies ; from valuable privileges ; from breach of vows, &c. : *Fourth*, Making earnest supplication for the pardon of sin, and peace with God, through the blood of the atonement, with all its important and happy fruits ; for the Spirit of sanctification, and abundant supplies of the grace that is necessary to the discharge of our duty ; for support and comfort, under all the trials to which we are liable, as we are sinful and mortal ; and for all temporal mercies that may be necessary, in our passage through this valley of tears : always remembering to view them as flowing in the channel of covenant love, and intended to be subservient to the preservation and progress of the spiritual life: *Fifth*, Pleading from every principle warranted in Scripture; from our own necessity; the all-sufficiency of God; the merit and intercession of our Saviour; and the glory of God in the comfort and happiness of his people: *Sixth*, Intercession for others, including the whole world of mankind; the kingdom of Christ, or his church universal; the church or churches with which we are more particularly connected; the interest of human society in general, and in that community to which we immediately belong; all that are invested with civil authority; the ministers of the everlasting gospel; and the rising generation: with whatever else, more particular, may seem necessary, or suitable, to the interest of that congregation where divine worship is celebrated.

III. Prayer after sermon, ought generally to have a relation to the subject that has been treated of in the discourse; and all other public prayers, to the circumstances that gave occasion for them.

IV. It is easy to perceive, that in all the preceding directions there is a very great compass and variety; and it is committed to the judgment and fidelity of the officiating pastor to insist chiefly on such parts, or to take in more or less of the several parts, as he shall be led to by the aspect of Providence; the particular state of the congregation in which he officiates; or the disposition and exercise of his own heart at the time. But we think it necessary to observe, that although we do not approve, as is well known, of confining ministers to set or fixed forms of prayer for public worship; yet it is the indispensable duty of every minister, previously to his entering on his office, to prepare and qualify himself for this part of his duty, as well as for preaching. He ought, by a thorough acquaintance with the Holy Scriptures, by reading the best writers on the subject, by meditation, and by a life of communion with God in secret, to endeavour to acquire both the spirit and the gift of prayer. Not only so, but when he is to enter on particular acts of worship, he should endeavour to compose his spirit, and to digest his thoughts for prayer, that it may be performed with dignity and propriety, as well as to the profit of those who join in it; and that he may not disgrace that important service by mean, irregular, or extravagant effusions.

CHAPTER VI.

OF THE PREACHING OF THE WORD.

I. THE preaching of the word being an institution of God for the salvation of men, great attention should be paid to the manner of performing it. Every minister ought to give diligent application to it; and endeavour to prove himself a workman that needeth not to be ashamed; rightly dividing the word of truth.

II. The subject of a sermon should be some verse or verses of Scripture; and its object, to explain, defend and apply some part of the system of divine truth; or, to point out the nature, and state the bounds and obligation, of some duty. A text should not be merely a motto, but should fairly contain the doctrine proposed to be handled. It is proper also that large portions of Scripture be sometimes expounded, and particularly improved, for the instruction of the people in the meaning and use of the Sacred Oracles.

III. The method of preaching requires much study, meditation, and prayer. Ministers ought, in general, to prepare their sermons with care; and not to indulge themselves in loose, extemporary harangues; nor to serve God with that which cost them naught. They ought, however, to keep to the simplicity of the gospel; expressing themselves in language agreeable to Scripture, and level to the understanding of the meanest of their hearers; carefully avoiding ostentation, either of parts or learning. They ought also to adorn, by their lives, the doctrine which they teach; and to be examples to the believers, in word, in conversation, in charity, in spirit, in faith, in purity.

IV. As one primary design of public ordinances is to pay social acts of homage to the most high God, ministers ought to be careful not to make their sermons so long as to interfere with or exclude the more important duties of prayer and praise; but preserve a just proportion between the several parts of public worship

V. The sermon being ended, the minister is to pray, and return thanks to almighty God: then let a psalm be sung; a collection raised for the poor, or other purposes of the church; and the assembly dismissed with the apostolic benediction.

VI. It is expedient that no person be introduced to preach in any of the churches under our care, unless by the consent of the pastor or church session.

CHAPTER VII.

OF THE ADMINISTRATION OF BAPTISM.

I. Baptism is not to be unnecessarily delayed; nor to be administered, in any case, by any private person; but by a minister of Christ, called to be the steward of the mysteries of God.

II. It is usually to be administered in the church. in the presence of the congregation; and it is convenient that it be performed immediately after sermon.

III. After previous notice is given to the minister, the child to be baptized is to be presented, by one or both the parents, signifying their desire that the child may be baptized.

IV. Before baptism, let the minister use some words of instruction, respecting the instiration, nature, use, and ends of this ordinance; showing.

"That it is instituted by Christ; that it is a
"seal of the righteousness of faith: that the
"seed of the faithful have no less a right to this
"ordinance, under the gospel, than the seed of
"Abraham to circumcision, under the Old Tes-
"tament; that Christ commanded all nations
"to be baptized; that he blessed little child-
"ren, declaring that of such is the kingdom of
"heaven; that children are federally holy, and
"therefore ought to be baptized; that we are,
"by nature, sinful, guilty, and polluted, and
"have need of cleansing by the blood of Christ,
"and by the sanctifying influences of the
"Spirit of God."

The minister is also to exhort the parents to the careful performance of their duty: requiring,

"That they teach the child to read the word
"of God; that they instruct it in the principles
"of our holy religion, as contained in the Scrip-
"tures of the Old and New Testament; an
"excellent summary of which we have in the
"Confession of Faith of this church, and in
"the Larger and Shorter Catechisms of the
"Westminster Assembly, which are to be re-
"commended to them, as adopted by this
"church, for their direction and assistance, in
"the discharge of this important duty; that
"they pray with and for it; that they set an
"example of piety and godliness before it,

"and endeavour, by all the means of God's
"appointment, to bring up their child n the
"nurture and admonition of the Lord.'

V. Then the minister is to pray for a blessing to attend this ordinance; after which, calling the child by its name, he shall say,

"I baptize thee, in the name of the Father,
"and of the Son, and of the Holy Ghost."

As he pronounces these words, he is to baptize the child with water, by pouring or sprinkling it on the face of the child, without adding any other ceremony: and the whole shall be concluded with prayer.

Although it is proper that baptism be administered in the presence of the congregation; yet there may be cases when it will be expedient to administer this ordinance in private houses: of which the minister is to be the judge.

CHAPTER VIII.

OF THE ADMINISTRATION OF THE LORD'S SUPPER.

I. THE communion, or supper of the Lord, is to be celebrated frequently; but how often, may be determined by the minister and eldership of each congregation, as they may judge most for edification.

II. The ignorant and scandalous are not to be admitted to the Lord's supper.

III. It is proper that public notice should

be given to the congregation, at least the Sabbath before the administration of this ordinance, and that, either then, or on some day of the week, the people be instructed in its nature, and a due preparation for it; that all may come in a suitable manner to this holy feast.

IV. When the sermon is ended, the minister shall show,

"That this is an ordinance of Christ; by
" reading the words of institution, either from
" one of the evangelists, or from 1 Cor. xi. chap-
"ter; which, as to him may appear expedient,
" he may explain and apply; that it is to be
" observed in remembrance of Christ, to show
" forth his death till he come; that it is of ines-
" timable benefit, to strengthen his people
" against sin; to support them under troubles:
" to encourage and quicken them in duty; to
" inspire them with love and zeal; to increase
" their faith, and holy resolution; and to beget
" peace of conscience, and comfortable hopes
" of eternal life."

He is to warn the profane, the ignorant, and scandalous, and those that secretly indulge themselves in any known sin, not to approach the holy table. On the other hand, he shall invite to this holy table, such as, sensible of their lost and helpless state of sin, depend upon the atonement of Christ for pardon and acceptance with God; such as, being instructed in the gospel doctrine, have a competent knowledge to discern the Lord's body, and such as desire to renounce their sins, and are determined to lead a holy and godly life.

V. The table, on which the elements are placed, being decently covered, the bread in convenient dishes, and the wine in cups, and the communicants orderly and gravely sitting around the table, (or in their seats before it,) in the presence of the minister; let him set the elements apart, by prayer and thanksgiving.

The bread and wine being thus set apart by prayer and thanksgiving, the minister is to take the bread, and break it, in the view of the people, saying, in expressions of this sort :—

"Our Lord Jesus Christ, on the same night
" in which he was betrayed, having taken bread,
" and blessed and broken it, gave it to his dis-
" ciples; as I, ministering in his name, give this
" bread unto you; saying, [here the bread is to
" be distributed] Take, eat: this is my body,
" which is broken for you: this do in remem-
" brance of me."

After having given the bread, he shall take the cup, and say—

"After the same manner our Saviour also
" took the cup; and having given thanks, as
" hath been done in his name, he gave it to
" the disciples; saying, [while the minister is
" repeating these words let him give the cup]
" This cup is the new testament in my blood,
" which is shed for many, for the remission of
" sins: drink ye all of it '

The minister himself is to communicate, at such time as may appear to him most convenient.

The minister may, in a few words, put the communicants in mind—

"Of the grace of God, in Jesus Christ, held "forth in this sacrament; and of their obliga- "tion to be the Lord's; and may exhort them "to walk worthy of the vocation wherewith they "are called; and, as they have professedly "received Christ Jesus the Lord, that they be "careful so to walk in him, and to maintain "good works."

It may not be improper for the minister to give a word of exhortation also to those who have been only spectators, reminding them—

"Of their duty; stating their sin and danger, "by living in disobedience to Christ, in neg- "lecting this holy ordinance; and calling upon "them to be earnest in making preparation for "attending upon it, at the next time of its cele- "bration."

Then the minister is to pray and give thanks to God.

"For his rich mercy, and invaluable good- "ness, vouchsafed to them in that sacred com- "munion; to implore pardon for the defects "of the whole service; and to pray for the ac- "ceptance of their persons and performances; "for the gracious assistance of the Holy Spirit, "to enable them, as they have received Christ "Jesus the Lord, so to walk in him; that they "may hold fast that which they have received, that no man take their crown; that their conversation may be as becometh the gospel; that they may bear about with them, continually, the dying of the Lord Jesus, that the life also of Jesus may be manifested in their mortal body; that their light may so shine before men, that others, seeing their good works, may glorify their Father who is in heaven."

The collection for the poor, and to defray the expense of the elements, may be made after this; or at such other time as may seem meet to the eldership.

Now let a psalm or hymn be sung, and the congregation dismissed, with the following or some other gospel benediction:

"Now the God of peace, that brought again from the dead our Lord Jesus, that great Shepherd of the sheep, through the blood of the everlasting covenant, make you perfect in every good work to do his will, working in you that which is well-pleasing in his sight, through Jesus Christ; to whom be glory for ever and ever. *Amen.*"

VI. As it has been customary, in some parts of our church, to observe a fast before the Lord's supper; to have a sermon on Saturday and Monday; and to invite two or three ministers on such occasions; and as these seasons have been blessed to many souls, and may tend to keep up a stricter union of ministers and congregations; we think it not improper that they who choose it may continue in this practice.

CHAPTER IX.

OF THE ADMISSION OF PERSONS TO SEALING ORDINANCES.

1. CHILDREN, born within the pale of the visible church, and dedicated to God in baptism, are under the inspection and government of the church; and are to be taught to read and repeat the catechism, the apostles' creed, and the Lord's prayer. They are to be taught to pray, to abhor sin, to fear God, and to obey the Lord Jesus Christ. And, when they come to years of discretion, if they be free from scandal, appear sober and steady, and to have sufficient knowledge to discern the Lord's body, they ought to be informed it is their duty and their privilege to come to the Lord's supper.

II. The years of discretion, in young Christians, cannot be precisely fixed. This must be left to the prudence of the eldership. The officers of the church are the judges of the qualifications of those to be admitted to sealing ordinances; and of the time when it is proper to admit young Christians to them.

III Those who are to be admitted to sealing

ordinances, shall be examined as to their knowledge and piety.

IV. When unbaptized persons apply for admission into the church, they shall, in ordinary cases, after giving satisfaction with respect to their knowledge and piety, make a public profession of their faith, in the presence of the congregation; and thereupon be baptized.

CHAPTER X.

OF THE MODE OF INFLICTING AND REMOVING CENSURES.

I. THE power which Christ has given the rulers of his Church is for edification, and not destruction. When, therefore, a communicant shall have been found guilty of a fault deserving censure, the judicatory shall proceed with all tenderness, and restore the offending brother in the spirit of meekness, its members considering themselves, lest they also be tempted. Censure ought to be inflicted with great solemnity; that it may be the means of impressing the mind of the delinquent with a proper sense of his sin; and that, with the divine blessing, it may lead him to repentance.

II. When the judicatory has resolved to pass sentence, suspending a communicant from church privileges, the Moderator shall pronounce the sentence in the following form:

"Whereas you have been found guilty [*by your own confession, or by sufficient proof, as the case may be*] of the sin of [*here mention the particular offence*], we declare you suspended from the sacrament of the Lord's Supper, till you give satisfactory evidence of repentance."

To this shall be added such advice, admonition, or rebuke, as may be judged necessary; and the whole shall be concluded with prayer to Almighty God, that he would follow this act of discipline with his blessing. In general, such censure should be inflicted in the presence of the judicatory only; but, if the judicatory think it expedient to rebuke the offender publicly, this solemn suspension may be in the presence of the Church.

III. After a person has been thus suspended, the Minister and Elders should frequently converse with him, as well as pray for him in private, that it would please God to give him repentance. And, particularly on days preparatory to the dispensing of the Lord's Supper, the prayers of the Church should be offered up for those who have shut themselves out from this holy communion.

IV. When the judicatory shall be satisfied as to the reality of the repentance of any suspended member, he shall be allowed to profess his repentance, and be restored to fellowship, in the presence of the Session, or of the Church.

V. When a suspended person has failed to manifest repentance for his offence, and has continued in obstinate impenitence not less than a year, it may become the duty of the judicatory to excommunicate him without further trial. The design of excommunication is to operate upon the offender as a means of reclaiming him, to deliver the Church from the scandal of his offence, and to inspire all with fear by the example of his punishment.

VI. When a judgment of excommunication is to be executed, with or without previous suspension, it is proper that the sentence be publicly pronounced against the offender.

The Minister shall, therefore, at a regular meeting of the Church, make a brief statement of the several steps which have been taken, with respect to the offender, announcing that it has been found necessary to excommunicate him.

He shall begin by showing (from Matt. xviii. 15, 16, 17, 18; 1 Cor. v. 1, 2, 3, 4, 5) the power of the Church to cast out unworthy members, and shall briefly explain the nature, use, and consequences of this censure.

Then he shall pronounce the sentence in the following or like form, viz.:

"Whereas A. B. hath been, by sufficient proof, convicted of [*here insert the sin*], and after much admonition and prayer refuseth to hear the Church, and hath manifested no evidence of repentance; therefore, in the name, and by the authority, of the Lord Jesus Christ, I pronounce him to be excluded from the communion of this Church."

After which, prayer shall be made for the conviction and reformation of the excommunicated person, and for the establishment of all true believers.

But the judicatory may omit the publication of the excommunication, when it judges that there is sufficient reason for such omission.

VII. When an excommunicated person shall be so affected by his state as to be brought to repentance, and desires to be readmitted to the privileges of the Church, the Session of the Church which excommunicated him, having obtained, and placed on record, sufficient evidence of his sincere repentance and deep contrition, shall proceed to restore him, recording, in explicit terms, the grounds on which such conclusion has been reached.

The sentence of restoration shall be pronounced by the Minister, at a regular meeting of the Church on the Lord's Day, in the following words:

"Whereas A. B. has been excluded from the communion of the Church, but has now given satisfactory evidence of repentance; in the name of the Lord Jesus Christ, and by his authority, I declare him absolved from the sentence of excommunication formerly pronounced against him; and I do restore him to the communion of the Church, that he may be a partaker of all the benefits of the Lord Jesus, to his eternal salvation."

After which, he shall be commended to God in prayer.

VIII. Censures, other than suspension from church privileges, or excommunication, shall be inflicted in such mode as the judicatory may direct.

CHAPTER XI.

OF THE SOLEMNIZATION OF MARRIAGE.

I. MARRIAGE is not a sacrament; nor peculiar to the church of Christ. It is proper that every commonwealth, for the good of society, make laws to regulate marriage; which all citizens are bound to obey.

II. Christians ought to marry in the Lord: therefore it is fit that their marriage be solemnized by a lawful minister; that special instruction may be given them, and suitable prayers made, when they enter into this relation.

III. Marriage is to be between one man and one woman only: and they are not to be within the degrees of consanguinity or affinity prohibited by the word of God.

IV. The parties ought to be of such years

of discretion as to be capable of making their own choice: and if they be under age, or live with their parents, the consent of the parents or others, under whose care they are, ought to be previously obtained, and well certified to the minister, before he proceeds to solemnize the marriage.

V. Parents ought neither to compel their children to marry contrary to their inclinations, nor deny their consent without just and important reasons.

VI. Marriage is of a public nature. The welfare of civil society, the happiness of families, and the credit of religion, are deeply interested in it. Therefore the purpose of marriage ought to be sufficiently published a proper time previously to the solemnization of it. It is enjoined on all ministers to be careful that, in this matter, they neither transgress the laws of God, nor the laws of the community: and that they may not destroy the peace and comfort of families, they must be properly certified with respect to the parties applying to them, that no just objections lie against their marriage.

VII. Marriage must always be performed before a competent number of witnesses; and at any time, except on a day of public humiliation. And we advise that it be not on the Lord's day. And the minister is to give a certificate of the marriage when required

VIII When the parties present themselves

for marriage, the minister is to desire, if there is any person present who knows any lawful reason why these persons may not be joined together in the marriage relation. that they will now make it known, or ever after hold their peace.

No objections being made, he is then severally to address himself to the parties to be married, in the following or like words :

" You, the man, declare in the presence of
" God, that you do not know any reason, by
" precontract or otherwise, why you may not
" lawfully marry this woman."

Upon his declaring he does not, the minister shall address himself to the bride, in the same or similar terms :

" You, the woman, declare in the presence
" of God, that you do not know any reason, by
" precontract or otherwise, why you may not
" lawfully marry this man."

Upon her declaring she does not, he is to begin with prayer for the presence and blessing of God.

The minister shall then proceed to give them some instruction from the scriptures, respecting the institution and duties of this state, showing—

" That God hath instituted marriage for the
" comfort and happiness of mankind, in declar-
" ing a man shall forsake his father and mother,
" and cleave unto his wife; and that marriage
" is honourable in all ; that he hath appointed

DIRECTORY FOR WORSHIP. 519

"various duties, which are incumbent upon those who enter into this relation; such as, a high esteem and mutual love for one another; bearing with each other's infirmities and weaknesses, to which human nature is subject in its present lapsed state; to encourage each other under the various ills of life; to comfort one another in sickness; in honesty and industry to provide for each other's temporal support; to pray for and encourage one another in the things which pertain to God, and to their immortal souls; and to live together as the heirs of the grace of life."

Then the minister shall cause the bridegroom and bride to join their hands, and shall pronounce the marriage covenant, first to the man, in these words:

"You take this woman, whom you hold by the hand, to be your lawful and married wife; and you promise, and covenant, in the presence of God and these witnesses, that you will be unto her a loving and faithful husband, until you shall be separated by death."

The bridegroom shall express his consent, by saying, "Yes, I do."

Then the minister shall address himself to the woman, in these words:

"You take this man, whom you hold by the hand, to be your lawful and married husband: and you promise, and covenant in the presence of God and these witnesses, that you will be unto him a loving, faithful, and obe-

"dient wife until you shall be separated by "death."

The bride shall express her consent, by saying, "Yes, I do."

Then the minister is to say,

"I pronounce you husband and wife, accord-"ing to the ordinance of God; whom there-"fore God hath joined together let no man put "asunder."

After this the minister may exhort them in a few words, to the mutual discharge of their duty.

Then let him conclude with prayer suitable to the occasion.

Let the minister keep a proper register for the names of all persons whom he marries, and of the time of their marriage, for the perusal of all whom it may concern.

CHAPTER XII.

OF THE VISITATION OF THE SICK.

I. WHEN persons are sick, it is their duty, before their strength and understanding fail them, to send for their minister, and to make known to him, with prudence, their spiritual state; or to consult him on the concerns of their precious souls. And it is his duty to visit them, at their request, and to apply himself, with all tenderness and love, to administer spiritual good to their immortal souls.

II. He shall instruct the sick out of the scriptures, that diseases arise not out of the ground, nor do they come by chance; but that they are directed and sent by a wise and holy God, either for correction of sin, for the trial of grace, for improvement in religion, or for other important ends: and that they shall work together for good to all those who make a wise improvement of God's visitation, neither despising his chastening hand, nor fainting under his rebukes.

III. If the minister finds the sick person to be grossly ignorant, he shall instruct him in the nature of repentance and faith, and the way of acceptance with God, through the mediation and atonement of Jesus Christ.

IV. He shall exhort the sick to examine himself, to search his heart, and try his former ways, by the word of God; and shall assist him, by mentioning some of the obvious marks and evidences of sincere piety.

V. If the sick shall signify any scruple, doubt, or temptation, under which he labours, the minister must endeavour to resolve his doubts, and administer instruction and direction, as the case may seem to require.

VI. If the sick appear to be a stupid, thoughtless, and hardened sinner, he shall endeavour to awaken his mind; to arouse his conscience; to convince him of the evil and danger of sin, of the curse of the law, and the wrath of God due to sinners; to bring him to an humble and penitential sense of his iniquities; and to state before him the fulness of the grace and mercy of God, in and through the glorious Redeemer; the absolute necessity of faith and repentance in order to his being interested in the favour of God, or his obtaining everlasting happiness.

VII. If the sick person shall appear to have knowledge, to be of a tender conscience, and to have been endeavouring to serve God in uprightness, though not without many failings and sinful infirmities; or if his spirit be broken with a sense of sin, or through apprehensions of the want of the divine favour; then it will be proper to administer consolation and encouragement to him, by setting before him the freeness and riches of the grace of God, the all-sufficiency of the righteousness of Christ, and the supporting promises of the Gospel.

VIII. The minister must endeavour to guard the sick person against ill-grounded persuasions of the mercy of God, without a vital union to Christ; and against unreasonable fears of death, and desponding discouragements; against presumption upon his own goodness and merit, upon the one hand, and against despair of the mercy and grace of God in Jesus Christ, on the other.

IX. In one word, it is the minister's duty to administer to the sick person instruction, conviction, support, consolation, or encouragement, as his case may seem to require.

At a proper time, when he is most composed, the minister shall pray with and for him.

X. Lastly, the minister may improve the present occasion to exhort those about the sick, to consider their mortality; to turn to the Lord and make their peace with him; in health to prepare for sickness, death and judgment.

CHAPTER XIII.

OF THE BURIAL OF THE DEAD.

I. When any person departs this life, let the corpse be taken care of in a decent manner; and be kept a proper and sufficient time before interment.

II. When the season for the funeral comes, let the dead body be decently attended to the grave, and interred. During such solemn occasions, let all who attend conduct themselves with becoming gravity; and apply themselves to serious meditation or discourse: and the minister, if present, may exhort them to consider the frailty of life, and the importance of being prepared for death and eternity.

CHAPTER XIV.

OF FASTING, AND OF THE OBSERVATION OF THE DAYS OF THANKSGIVING.

1. THERE is no day under the gospel commanded to be kept holy, except the Lord's day, which is the Christian Sabbath.

II. Nevertheless, to observe days of fasting and thanksgiving, as the extraordinary dispensations of divine providence may direct, we judge both scriptural and rational.

III. Fasts and thanksgivings may be observed by individual Christians; or families, in private; by particular congregations; by a number of congregations contiguous to each other; by the congregations under the care of a presbytery, or of a synod; or by all the congregations of our church.

IV. It must be left to the judgment and discretion of every Christian and family to determine when it is proper to observe a private fast or thanksgiving; and to the church-sessions to determine for particular congregations, and to the presbyteries or synods to determine for larger districts. When it is deemed expedient that a fast or thanksgiving should be general, the call for them must be judged of by the synod or General Assembly. And if at any time the civil power should think it proper to appoint a fast or thanksgiving, it is the duty of the ministers and people of our communion, as we live under a Christian government, to pay all due respect to the same.

V. Public notice is to be given a convenient time before the day of fasting or thanksgiving comes, that persons may so order their temporal affairs, that they may properly attend to the duties thereof.

VI There shall be public worship upon all

such days: and let the prayers, psalms, portions of Scripture to be read, and sermons, be all in a special manner adapted to the occasion.

VII. On fast days, let the minister point out the authority and providences calling to the observation thereof; and let him spend a more than usual portion of time in solemn prayer, particular confession of sin, especially of the sins of the day and place, with their aggravations, which have brought down the judgments of heaven. And let the whole day be spent in deep humiliation and mourning before God.

VIII. On days of thanksgiving, he is to give the like information respecting the authority and providences which call to the observance of them; and to spend a more than usual part of the time in the giving of thanks, agreeably to the occasion, and in singing psalms or hymns of praise.

It is the duty of people on these days to rejoice with holy gladness of heart; but let trembling be so joined with our mirth, that no excess or unbecoming levity be indulged.

CHAPTER XV.

THE DIRECTORY FOR SECRET AND FAMILY WORSHIP.

I. BESIDES the public worship in congregations, it is the indispensable duty of each person, alone, in secret; and of every family, by itself in private, to pray to, and worship God.

II. Secret worship is most plainly enjoined by our Lord. In this duty every one, apart by himself, is to spend some time in prayer, reading the Scriptures, holy meditation, and serious self-examination. The many advantages arising from a conscientious discharge of these duties, are best known to those who are found in the faithful discharge of them.

III. Family worship, which ought to be performed by every family, ordinarily morning and evening, consists in prayer, reading the Scriptures, and singing praises.

IV. The head of the family, who is to lead in this service, ought to be careful that all the members of his household duly attend; and that none withdraw themselves unnecessarily from any part of family worship; and that all refrain from their common business while the Scriptures are read, and gravely attend to the same, no less than when prayer or praise is offered up.

V. Let the heads of families be careful to instruct their children and servants in the principles of religion. Every proper opportunity ought to be embraced for such instruction. But we are of opinion, that the Sabbath evenings, after public worship, should be sacredly preserved for this purpose. Therefore we highly disapprove of paying unnecessary private visits on the Lord's day; admitting strangers into the families, except when necessity or charity requires it; or any other practices, whatever plausible pretences may be offered in their favour, if they interfere with the above important and necessary duty.

NOTE.—The following "General Rules for Judicatories," not having been submitted to the presbyteries, make no part of the Constitution of the Presbyterian Church. Yet the General Assembly of 1871, considering uniformity in proceedings in all the subordinate judicatories as greatly conducive to order and despatch in business, having revised and approved these rules, recommended them to all the lower judicatories of the Church for adoption.

APPENDIX.

GENERAL RULES FOR JUDICATORIES.
ADOPTED BY THE GENERAL ASSEMBLY IN 1871 AND AMENDED IN 1885.*

I. THE Moderator shall take the chair precisely at the hour to which the judicatory stands adjourned; and shall immediately call the members to order; and, on the appearance of a quorum, shall open the session with prayer.

II. If a quorum be assembled at the time appointed, and the Moderator be absent, the last Moderator present, *being a commissioner*, or if there be none, the senior member present, shall be requested to take his place without delay, until a new election.

III. If a quorum be not assembled at the hour appointed, any two members shall be competent to adjourn from time to time, that an opportunity may be given for a quorum to assemble.

IV. It shall be the duty of the Moderator, at all times, to preserve order, and to endeavor to conduct all business before the judicatory to a speedy and proper result.

V. It shall be the duty of the Moderator, carefully to keep notes of the several articles of business which may be assigned for particular days, and to call them up at the time appointed.

* See note on preceding page.

VI. The Moderator may speak to points of order, in preference to other members, rising from his seat for that purpose; and shall decide questions of order, subject to an appeal to the judicatory by any two members.

VII. The Moderator shall appoint all committees, except in those cases in which the judicatory shall decide otherwise. In appointing the standing committees, the Moderator may appoint a Vice-Moderator, who may occupy the chair at his request, and otherwise assist him in the discharge of his duties.

VIII. When a vote is taken by ballot in any judicatory, the Moderator shall vote with the other members; but he shall not vote in any other case, unless the judicatory be equally divided; when, if he do not choose to vote, the question shall be lost.

IX. The person first named on any committee shall be considered as the chairman thereof, whose duty it shall be to convene the committee; and, in case of his absence or inability to act, the second named member shall take his place and perform his duties.

X. It shall be the duty of the clerk, as soon as possible after the commencement of the sessions of every judicatory, to form a complete roll of the members present, and put the same into the hands of the Moderator. And it shall also be the duty of the clerk, whenever any additional members take their seats, to add their names, in their proper places, to the said roll.

XI. It shall be the duty of the clerk immediately to file all papers, in the order in which they have been read, with proper indorsements,

GENERAL RULES FOR JUDICATORIES. 531

and to keep them in perfect order. The Stated Clerk shall receive all overtures, memorials and miscellaneous papers addressed to the judicatory; shall make record of the same and deliver them to the Committee on Bills and Overtures for appropriate disposition or reference. This committee shall have the floor on the reassembling of the judicatory after each adjournment to report its recommendations as to orders of business or reference of papers, and this right of the committee shall take precedence of the Orders of the Day.

XII. The minutes of the last meeting of the judicatory shall be presented at the commencement of its sessions, and, if requisite, read and corrected.

XIII. Business left unfinished at the last sitting is ordinarily to be taken up first.

XIV. A motion made must be seconded, and afterwards repeated by the Moderator, or read aloud, before it is debated; and every motion shall be reduced to writing, if the Moderator or any member require it.

XV. Any member who shall have made a motion, shall have liberty to withdraw it, with the consent of his second, before any debate has taken place thereon; but not afterwards, without the leave of the judicatory.

XVI. If a motion under debate contain several parts, any two members may have it divided, and a question taken on each part.

XVII. When various motions are made with respect to the filling of blanks, with particular numbers or times, the question shall always be first taken on the highest number and the longest time.

XVIII. Motions to lay on the table, to take up business, to adjourn, and the call for the previous question, shall be put without debate. On questions of order, postponement, or commitment, no member shall speak more than once. On all other questions, each member may speak twice, but not oftener, without express leave of the judicatory.

XIX. When a question is under debate, no motion shall be received, unless to adjourn, to lay on the table, to postpone indefinitely, to postpone to a day certain, to commit, or to amend; which several motions shall have precedence in the order in which they are herein arranged; and the motion for adjournment shall always be in order.

XX. An amendment, and also an amendment to an amendment, may be moved on any motion; but a motion, to amend an amendment to an amendment, shall not be in order. Action on amendments shall precede action on the original motion. A substitute shall be treated as an amendment.

XXI. A distinction shall be observed between a motion to lay on the table *for the present*, and a motion to lay on the table *unconditionally*, viz.: A motion to lay on the table, *for the present*, shall be taken without debate; and, if carried in the affirmative, the effect shall be to place the subject on the docket, and it may be taken up and considered at any subsequent time. But a motion to lay on the table, *unconditionally*, shall be taken without debate; and, if carried in the affirmative, it shall not be in order to take up the subject during the same meeting of the judicatory, without a vote of reconsideration.

GENERAL RULES FOR JUDICATORIES. 533

XXII. The previous question shall be put in this form, namely, Shall the main question be now put? It shall only be admitted when demanded by a majority of the members present; and the effect shall be to put an end to all debate and bring the body to a direct vote: First, on a motion to commit the subject under consideration (if such motion shall have been made); secondly, if the motion for commitment does not prevail, on pending amendments; and lastly, on the main question.

XXIII. A question shall not be again called up or reconsidered at the same sessions of the judicatory at which it has been decided, unless by the consent of two-thirds of the members who were present at the decision; and unless the motion to reconsider be made and seconded, by persons who voted with the majority.

XXIV. A subject which has been indefinitely postponed, either by the operation of the previous question, or by a motion for indefinite postponement, shall not be again called up during the same sessions of the judicatory, unless by the consent of three-fourths of the members who were present at the decision.

XXV. Members ought not, without weighty reasons, to decline voting, as this practice might leave the decision of very interesting questions to a small proportion of the judicatory. Silent members, unless excused from voting, must be considered as acquiescing with the majority.

XXVI. When the Moderator has commenced taking the vote, no further debate or remark shall be admitted, unless there has evidently been a mistake, in which case the mistake shall be rectified, and the Moderator shall recommence taking the vote. If the house shall pass the motion to "vote on a given subject at a time named," speeches shall thereafter be limited to ten minutes. When the time named shall arrive no further discussion shall be allowed either as explanation or argument, but the Moderator shall proceed to put to vote in their proper order all pending propositions, and also all those of which notice has been given during the discussion. Should the hour for adjournment or recess arrive during the voting, it shall be postponed to finish the vote, unless the majority shall vote to adjourn; in which case the voting shall on the reassembling of the house take precedence of all other business till it is finished. Under this rule "the yeas and nays" shall not be called except on the final motion to adopt as a whole. This motion to fix a time for voting shall be put without debate.

XXVII. The yeas and nays on any question shall not be recorded, unless required by one-third of the members present. If division is called for on any vote, it shall be by a rising vote without a count. If on such a rising vote the Moderator is unable to decide, or a quorum rise to second a call for "tellers," then the vote shall be taken by rising, and the count made by tellers, who shall pass through the aisles and report to the Moderator the number voting on each side.

XXVIII. No member, in the course of debate, shall be allowed to indulge in personal reflections.

XXIX. If more than one member rise to

speak at the same time, the member who is most distant from the Moderator's chair shall speak first. In the discussion of all matters where the sentiment of the house is divided, it is proper that the floor should be occupied alternately by those representing the different sides of the question.

XXX. When more than three members of the judicatory shall be standing at the same time, the Moderator shall require all to take their seats, the person only excepted who may be speaking.

XXXI. Every member, when speaking, shall address himself to the Moderator, and shall treat his fellow-members, and especially the Moderator, with decorum and respect.

XXXII. No speaker shall be interrupted, unless he be out of order; or for the purpose of correcting mistakes, or misrepresentations.

XXXIII. Without express permission, no member of a judicatory, while business is going on, shall engage in private conversation; nor shall members address one another, nor any person present, but through the Moderator.

XXXIV. It is indispensable, that members of ecclesiastical judicatories maintain great gravity and dignity while judicially convened; that they attend closely in their speeches to the subject under consideration, and avoid prolix and desultory harangues; and, when they deviate from the subject, it is the privilege of any member, and the duty of the Moderator, to call them to order.

XXXV. If any member act, in any respect, in a disorderly manner, it shall be the privilege of any member, and the duty of the Moderator, to call him to order.

XXXVI. If any member consider himself aggrieved by a decision of the Moderator, it shall be his privilege to appeal to the judicatory, and the question on the appeal shall be taken without debate.

XXXVII. No member shall retire from any judicatory without the leave of the Moderator, nor withdraw from it to return home without the consent of the judicatory.

XXXVIII. All judicatories have a right to sit in private, on business, which in their judgment ought not to be matter of public speculation.

XXXIX. Besides the right to sit judicially in private, whenever they think proper to do so, all judicatories have a right to hold what are commonly called "interlocutory meetings," in which members may freely converse together, without the formalities which are usually necessary in judicial proceedings.

XL. Whenever a judicatory is about to sit in a judicial capacity, it shall be the duty of the Moderator solemnly to announce, from the chair, that the body is about to pass to the consideration of the business assigned for trial, and to enjoin on the members to recollect and regard their high character as judges of a court of Jesus Christ, and the solemn duty in which they are about to act.

XLI. In all cases before a judicatory, where there is an accuser or prosecutor, it is expedient that there be a committee of the judicatory appointed (provided the number of members be

GENERAL RULES FOR JUDICATORIES. 537

sufficient to admit it without inconvenience), who shall be called the "Judicial Committee," and whose duty it shall be to digest and arrange all the papers, and to prescribe, under the direction of the judicatory, the whole order of proceedings. The members of this committee shall be entitled, notwithstanding their performance of this duty, to sit and vote in the cause, as members of the judicatory.

XLII. But in cases of process on the ground of general rumor, where there is, of course, no particular accuser, there may be a committee appointed (if convenient), who shall be called the "Committee of Prosecution," and who shall conduct the whole course on the part of the prosecution. The members of this committee shall not be permitted to sit in judgment in the case.

XLIII. The permanent officers of a judicatory shall have the rights of corresponding members in matters touching their several offices.

XLIV. The Moderator of every judicatory above the Church Session, in finally closing its sessions, in addition to prayer, may cause to be sung, an appropriate psalm or hymn, and shall pronounce the apostolical benediction.

SUPPLEMENTARY INDEX

TO BOOK OF DISCIPLINE AND CHAPTER X., DIRECTORY OF WORSHIP.

[Figures, thus (28), refer to sections of Book of Discipline, and thus (II.), to sections of Chap. X. Dir. of Worship.]

ABSENTEES, names to be noted, 28.
roll of, 49.
certificate of dismission of, 116.
Accusations, caution against, 13.
Accused person, private conference with, 9.
copy of charges for, 19.
refusal to obey citation, 19.
time for appearance, 21.
non-appearance of, 21.
counsel for, 21, 22.
notice of examination of witnesses, 23.
may be kept from communion, 32.
non-exercise of office by, 32.
suspension for contumacy, 33.
cited twice if necessary, 21, 33.
self, action in case of, 47.
Admonition, 34, 40.
in appeals, 100.
Affirmation, how administered, 61.
Appeal, from decision of Moderator, 27.
heard without debate, 27.
to be recorded, 27.
Appeals, entry on minutes, 24.
record to be transmitted, 24.
in cases without process, 47.
new evidence during prosecution of, 69.
and complaints consolidated, 93.
definition of, 94.
in general, 94–102.

Appeals, parties in, 94.
grounds of, 95.
notice of, when and how given, 96.
specification of errors, 96, 99.
records in, lodgment of, 96, 97, 101.
time of lodgment of, 97.
counsel in, 97.
abandonment of, 97.
parties may not vote, 93, 98.
vote in, 99 (5).
judgment in, 99.
new trial in, 99.
entertainment of, 99.
order of proceedings in, 99.
minute, explanatory of judgment, 100.
effect of judgment upon, 100.
taken to next judicatory, 102.
Appellant, name given, 94.
time of appearance, 97.
counsel for, 97.
must lodge appeal, 97.
abandoning appeal, 97.
may not vote, 98.
hearing of, 99 (2).
Appellee, 94.

BAPTIZED children as church members, 5.
included in certificates of dismission, 114.
Baptized persons all church members, 5.

CANDIDATE, certificate of dismission, how long valid, 115.
must be reported, 115.

(538)

SUPPLEMENTARY INDEX. 539

Cases with process, general rules, 18–32.
  before session, 33–35.
  before presbytery, 36–46.
  without process, 47–53.
  delay in, 47.
  judgment and record in, 47.
Censures, infliction and removal of, 30.
  by session, names of, 34.
  in case of ministers, 40.
  cautions with regard to, 41.
  of witness for contumacy, 67.
  of records, how to be recorded, 74.
  for failure to send up records in complaints, 92.
  in appeals, 101.
  design of, 1.
  manner of, I.
  sentence in, form of, II.
  may be public, II.
  mode of, VIII.
Certificates of dismission, church members, 109.
  ministers, 44, 51, 110, 111.
  extinct church, 112.
  extinct presbytery, 113.
  time limit, church member, 114.
  ministers, etc., 115.
Charges, in general, 15–17.
  entry on minutes, 24.
  reading of, 19.
  copy of, for accused, 19.
  objections to, 22.
  amendments to, 22.
  refusal to answer, 33.
  proved by one witness, 58.
  proof of specifications, 58.
Children baptized.—See *Baptized Children.*
Church, proceedings of, report to session, 71.
  review by session, 71.
  on records of session, 71.
Church extinct, members of, status of, 112.
  session of, cases of discipline, 112.
Church members, who are, 5.
  suspended, roll of, 49.
  jurisdiction over, 108, 109.
  dismissed, status of, 109.
  removals of, 114.

Church members must have certificate of dismission, 114.
  baptized children of, 114.
  certificate of, how long valid, 114.
  reception to be reported, 114.
  absentee, 49, 116.
  censured, conduct towards, III.
  suspended, repentance of, IV.
  suspended and unrepentant, V.
  excommunication of, VI.
  restoration of, VII., IV.—See, also, *Communicants.*
Citations, issuing of, 19.
  service of, 20.
  refusal to obey, 21.
  second, 21, 33.
  third, of ministers, 38.
Clerk, to sign citations, 19.
  authenticate records, 63.
  receive testimony, 65.
  action of, in complaints, 84, 86.
  action of, in appeals, 96.
Commissions to take testimony, 65.
  how appointed, 65.
  rules for, 65.
  competency of testimony before, 65.
  transmission of testimony before, 65.
Commissions, Judicial.—See *Judicial.*
Communicants, withdrawal of, not under charges, 48.
  absent without certificate, 49.
  separate roll of absentee, 49.
  in neglect of church ordinances, 50.
  joining other denominations, 52.
Complainant, name given, 89.
  hearing of, 87.
  must lodge complaint, 86.
  may not vote, 90.
  may appeal, 91.
Complaints, definition of, 83.
  notice of, when and how given, 84.
  time of lodgment, with higher judicatory, 84, 86.
  effect of, in cases non-judicial, 85.

Complaints, order of proceedings before judicatory, 88.
 in judicial cases, order of proceedings, 87.
 effect of, if sustained, 88.
 parties to, 89.
 counsel in, 89.
 parties may not vote, 90.
 parties may appeal, 91.
 records in case of, to be sent up, 84, 92.
 appeal and, consolidated, 93.
Control, review and, 70–76.
Contumacy, 21.
 in cases before sessions, 33.
 of ministers, 38.
 of witnesses, 65.
Corrupt practices, neglect of, by judicatory, 76.
Counsel, in absence of accused, 21, 22.
 for either party, 26.
 must be communicants, 26.
 may not vote or judge, 26.
 in appeals, 97.
DEACONS, general rules for trial of, 46.
 tried by session, 46.
 lose office by dismission, 109.
Decision.—See *Judicial Decision.*
Demission of ministry, 51.
Deposition, 34, 40.
 cautions in cases of, 41.
 restoration after, 43.
Discipline, in general, 1–5.
 definition of, 1.
 ends of, 2.
 subjects of, 5.
 cases of, before extinct session, 112.
 before extinct Presbytery, 113.
Dismission.—See *Certificates of Dismission.*
Dismission, jurisdiction in cases of, 109–113.
Dissents, in general, 103–107.
 definition of, 103.
 form of, 105.
 entry on records, 105.
 parties to, 107.
ELDERS, jurisdiction over, 18.
 acting, general rules for trial of, 46.
 lose office by dismission, 109.

Errors, to be carefully considered, 41.
Evidence, introduction of, 23.
 in rebuttal, 23.
 new, 23.
 filing of, 24.
 questions of, 27.
 care in receiving, 54.
 kinds of, 59.
 records of judicatory as, 63.
 testimony before judicatories as, 64.
 new, after trial, 68.
 new, during prosecution of appeal, 69.
Exceptions, 25.
Excommunication, by whom inflicted, 34, 40.
 not without process, 50.
 design of, V.
 time-limit, V.
 sentence of, VI.
 publication of, VI.
 omission of publication of, VI.
 form of, VI.
 restoration from, VII.
GENERAL ASSEMBLY, ministers in trans., 110.
HERESY, may call for deposition, 41.
 neglect of, by judicatory, 76.
INFIRMITY, acts of, 41.
Investigations, to be speedy, 32, 45.
JUDGMENT, entering of, 23.
 entry on minutes, 24.
 transmission to higher judicatory, 29.
 in cases without process. 47.
 in appeals, 99, 100.
Judicatories, jurisdiction of, 18.
 first meeting of, 19.
 objections to, 22.
 private session of, 23.
 minutes of, 24.
 may sit with closed doors, 31.
 removing ministers to restore, 43.
 power of, in cases without process, 47.
 offence in presence of, 47.
 may decide competency of witnesses, 55.
 records of, as evidence, 64.

SUPPLEMENTARY INDEX. 541

Judicatories, testimony before, as evidence before others, 64.
may appoint commission to take testimony, 65.
members of, may be witnesses, 66.
neglect of duty by, 76.
may answer protests, 106.
Judicatory, higher, power over lower:
in neglect of process, 18.
in records, 71, 72.
in irregular proceedings, 74.
in unconstitutional proceedings, 75.
in neglect of duty, 76.
pending production of record, 92.
Judicatory, lower, unconstitutional proceedings, 75.
neglect of duty, 76.
obliged to send records, 71, 92.
action upon judgment of, in appeals, 99.
Judicial cases, complaint in, 87.
decision, must be regularly reviewed, 74.
may be submitted to commission, 118.
Judicial commission, may be appointed, 118.
only by Assembly and Synod, 118.
number of members, 118.
decisions of, 118.
review of decisions of, 118.
place of sitting, 118.
findings to be entered on minutes, 118.
Jurisdiction, in process, 18.
objections to, 22.
church-members, 108 109.
ministers, 108, 110.

LICENTIATE, certificate of dismission, how long valid, 115.
must be reported, 109.
Limitations of time, 114–117.

MEMBERS.—See *Church-Members*.
Ministers, jurisdiction over, 18.
general rules for trial of, 36–45.
charges against, to be well weighed, 36.

Ministers, offences of, outside bounds of home presbytery, 37.
counsel for, 38.
third citation of, 38.
contumacy of, 38.
suspension of, from communion, 38, 40.
from office, 38, 40.
censures to be inflicted on, 40.
suspension of, followed by deposition, 40.
complaints against, for slight offences, 42.
restoration of, personal conditions, 43.
duty of presbytery, 43.
deposition of, if pastors, 44.
suspension of, if pastors, 44.
pulpits declared vacant, 44.
letter for deposed, 44.
accused, to refrain from exercise of office, 45.
demission of, 51.
abandoning the ministry, 53.
becoming independent, 53.
joining other denominations, 53.
joining heretical denominations, 53.
jurisdiction over, 108.
dismissed, jurisdiction over, 110.
status of, 110.
in transitu, 110.
certificates of dismission of, 44, 51, 110, 111.
must specify particular body, 113.
certificates, how long valid, 115.
reception to be reported, 115.
duty in excommunications, VI.
Minutes of judicatory, 24.
Moderator to decide questions of order and evidence, 27.
to sign citations, 19.
to authenticate records, 63.
to receive complaints, 84.
to receive appeals, 96.

OATH, how administered, 61.
Objections, 22.
Offences, definition of, 8.
to be set forth by charge, 15.

SUPPLEMENTARY INDEX.

Offences, in presence of judicatory, 47.
in case of self-accused persons, 47.
of ministers, 36.
jurisdiction in, 108.
limit of time for prosecution of, 117.
Order of proceedings, objections to, 22.
questions of, 27.

PARTIES, injured, as prosecutors, 8.
original, in prosecution, 10.
heard on objections, 22.
may introduce new witnesses, 23.
excluded from private session, 23.
may take exceptions, 25.
may have counsel, 26.
consent of, to vote of absentees, 28.
copies of record for, 29.
as witnesses, 55.
relationship to, affects witnesses, 56.
how examine witnesses, 60.
may have questions recorded, 62.
may ask commission, 65.
consent of, for new evidence, 69.
hearing of, in complaints, 87.
names of, in complaints, 89.
may not vote in complaints, 90.
may appeal, 91.
may not vote in appeals, 98.
hearing of, in appeals, 99.
Pastors.—See *Ministers*.
Personal injury, conditions in cases of, 8, 17.
Pleas, 22.
entry on minutes, 24.
Prayer, for suspended members, III.
for excommunicated persons, VI.
Presbytery, jurisdiction of, in process, 18.
duty towards ministers, 36.
duty towards other presbyteries in cases of ministers, 37.

Presbytery, duty of, in restoration of ministers, 43.
duty to ministers deposed without excommunication, 44.
proceedings subject to review, 70.
jurisdiction of, over dismissed ministers, 110.
jurisdiction over members of extinct church, 111.
over cases of discipline of extinct church, 111.
extinct, status of members of, 113.
Private session, 23, 31.
Proceedings, irregular, must be corrected, 74.
unconstitutional action of judicatory in, 75.
Process, judicial, object of, 4.
parties in cases of, 6–14.
general rules, 18–32.
neglect of, by lower judicatory, 18.
objections to order of, 22.
Process, cases without, 47–53.
delay in, 47.
judgment and record in, 47.
Prosecution, unavailing, 7.
conditions of, individuals, 8.
judicatories, 9.
initiation of, by judicatories, 10.
committee of, 11.
limit of time for, 117.
Prosecutor, warning to, 14.
Protests, in general, 103–107.
definition of, 104.
form of, 105.
entry of, on records, 105.
answer to, 106.
modification of, 106.
parties to, 107.

QUESTIONS of order and evidence, 27.
irrelevant or frivolous, 60, 65.
leading, 60.
to be recorded, 62.

REBUKE, 34, 40.
Record of the case, what it is, 24.
transmission to higher judicatory, 24, 29.

SUPPLEMENTARY INDEX. 543

Records, nothing else to be considered, 24.
copies for parties, 29.
of proceedings in case of reference, 82.
to be read in complaints, 87.
to be read in appeals, 99 (1).
of session, 71.
how often to be reviewed, 71.
omission to send up, 72.
of lower judicatory, required to be produced, 71.
members of judicatory not to vote on review of, 73.
in case of complaint must be sent up, 92.
in appeal must be sent up, 101.
Reference in general, 77–82.
definition, 77.
subjects of, 78.
object of, 79.
effect of, upon cases, 79.
members of lower judicatory may vote, 80.
judgment in case of, *not final*, 81.
record of proceedings in, 82.
Removals, 114–116.
Respondent, 89.
Restoration of church-members, IV., VII.
ministers, 43.
Review and control, general, 70–76.
frequency of, 71.
right of, 70.
order of proceedings in, 72.
members of judicatory not to vote on, 73.
censure to be recorded, and how, 74.
irregular proceedings must be corrected, 74.
Roll of absentee members, 49.
suspended members, 49.
Roll-call of judicatory in trial, 28.

Schism may call for deposition, 41.
Self-accused person, case of, 47.
Sentence, form of, in censures, II.
in excommunications, VI.
in restoration, VII.
publication of, 35, II., VI.

Session, jurisdiction of, in process, 18.
censures by, names of, 34.
special rules for cases before, 33–35.
cases without process, 48, 49, 50, 52.
proceedings subject to review, 70.
report of church proceedings to, 71.
records of, to include church proceedings, 71.
review of church proceedings by, 71.
jurisdiction of, over dismissed members, 109.
of extinct church, case of discipline, 112.
Slander, investigation of, 12.
record may conclude, 12.
Specifications, 15–17.
reading of, 19.
copy of, for accused, 19.
objections to, 22.
amendments to, 22.
entry on minutes, 24.
proof of two may prove charge, 58.
Suspended members. — See *Church-Members.*
Suspension, 33, 34, 38, 40, 50.
may be public, II.
Synod, proceedings of, review of, 70.
jurisdiction of, over members of extinct presbytery, 113.
jurisdiction over cases of discipline in extinct presbytery, 113.

Testimony, reception of, 54.
record of, 63.
before a judicatory as evidence before another, 64.
commissioners to take, 65.
record of, before commission, 65.
of member of judicatory, 66.
new, in appeals, 69.
improper, 95.
See also *Evidence* and *Witnesses.*
Time, limitations of, 114–117.
Trials, order of procedure, 19, 22, 23.

Trials, to be speedy, 32, 45.
  new, 68, 69.
  new, in appeals, 99.

VOTE, on several charges, 16.
  qualifications for, 28.
  not allowed to persons under process, 39.
  member of judicatory under review not to, 73.
  member of judicatory may on reference, 80.
  parties to complaint may not, 90.
  in appeals may not, 98.
  in appeals, 99 (5).

WITNESSES, names of, in specifications, 15.
  names of, for accused, 19.
  citations for, 19.

Witnesses, accused not to disclose names of, 19.
  time allowed for appearance of, 21.
  examination of, 23.
  new, 23.
  competent, 54, 55.
  incompetent, 55.
  credibility of, 56.
  husband or wife as, 57.
  charges proved by one, 58.
  presence of, during testimony, 59.
  how to be examined, 60.
  oath or affirmation of, 61.
  questions to, record of, 62.
  answers of, record of, 62.
  commission to examine, 65.
  members of judicatory may be, 66.
  contumacy of, 67.

GENERAL INDEX.

[For Supplementary Index to Book of Discipline and Chapter X., Directory for Worship, see page 538.]

A.
	PAGE
AMENDMENTS	532
Appeals on points of order	530, 536
in general	487
Assembly, General, of the	429
mode of dissolving	431
representation in	429, 492
commissioners to	431, 458

B.
Baptism, of the administration of	504
Bishops or pastors, of	412
election and ordination of	441
instalment	451
resignation	453

C.
Call, form of a	442
how subscribed	443
how to prosecute a	444
Candidates, of licensing	435
Certificates of dismission	491, 493
Charges	464
Children, baptized	410, 461
Church, of the	409
censures	470, 512
extinct	492

	PAGE
Church government, of	417
of the officers of the	411
ordinances in a particular	415
worship in a vacant church	457
Church members, who are	410, 461
reception of	420
jurisdiction over	420, 491
dismission of	491, 493
roll of absentee	475
suspension, etc.	475, 512
restoration of	515
Clerks, of	456, 530, 537
Commissioners to the General Assembly	431, 458
Committees	530, 531
Complaints	484
Congregations, vacant, assembling for worship	457
Counsel	463

D.

Deacons, of	414
of electing and ordaining	432
trials of	473
Dead, of the burial of the	523
Discipline, Book of	460
general principles of	460
index to	538
Dismission, jurisdiction in	491
Dissents	490
Division	534

E.

Elders, ruling, of	413
of electing and ordaining	432
trials of	473
Evidence	469, 477
Excommunication, of	470, 514

GENERAL INDEX. 547

F.

	PAGE
Family worship, directory for	525
Fasting, of the observation of the days of	523

G.

Government, Form of	405
preliminary principles of	405

I.

Instalment of pastor	451
Interlocutory meetings	536

J.

Judicatories, church, the several kinds of	415
closing services	537
general rules for	529
judicial sessions	536
jurisdiction of	491
private sessions	536
prosecution by	463
Judicial Commissions	428, 430, 494
Judicial Committee	536

L.

License, form of	439
Limitation of time in dismissions	493
Lord's Day, of the sanctification of the	495
Lord's Supper, of the administration of the	506

M.

Marriage, of the solemnization of	516
Minister, of the translation of	449
trial of	471, 476
See, also, *Bishops*.	
Ministry, demission of the	475
Missions, of	454
Moderators, of, 455, 465, 469, 479, 484, 487, 529, 534, 537	
how to be chosen	456

GENERAL INDEX.

        PAGE

Moderators, ministers, perpetual, of church sessions. 419
    of presbyteries, synods, and the General Assembly. 456
Motions 531

O.

Oath 475
Offences 461
Ordinances in a particular church 411, 415
Ordination, trials for 444
    mode of 445, 448
    questions proposed at 446

P.

Pastoral charge, resignation of a 453
Pastors. See *Bishops*.
Postponement 533
Prayer, of public 499
Preaching, of 502
Presbytery, of the 422
    extinct 492
Process, parties in 461
    cases without 474
    general rules 471
Prosecution, in general 462, 537
    limit of time 494
Protests, nature of 490
Psalms, singing of 496

Q.

Question, previous 533
Questions, consideration of 532
    of order 469, 532
Quorum, of a 419, 423, 427, 430, 529

R.

Reconsideration 533
References 483

	PAGE
Removals of candidates and licentiates	493
of a minister	449, 493
of church members	493
Resignation of a charge	453
Restoration	515
Review and control	481
Revision of records	481
Roll of suspended and absent members	475
Rules for Judicatories	529

S.

Sabbath, of the	495
Sacraments, to be dispensed only by an ordained minister	504
Scriptures, of public reading of the	497
Sealing ordinances, of admission to	511
Secret worship, directory for	526
Session, the church	419
cases before	470, 474
ministers moderators of	419
Sick, the visitation of the	520
Speakers and speaking	535
Synod, of the	427

T.

Testimony, of new	480
Thanksgiving, of the observation of the days of	524
Trials	471

V.

Vote, taking the	464, 480, 533, 534
persons not allowed to	472, 482, 486, 488

W.

Witnesses, of	477
Worship, the directory for	495
secret and family	525

www.ingramcontent.com/pod-product-compliance
Lightning Source LLC
Chambersburg PA
CBHW022129160426
43197CB00009B/1206